MP3 free download

초급교양영어

Freshman English 1

Second Edition

revised

Andrew Finch

KNU PRESS

Author: Dr. Andrew Finch is Professor of English Education in the Teachers' College of Kyungpook National University, where he teaches graduate and undergraduate pre-service and in-service teachers of English. His courses and teacher-training seminars include Classroom-based Assessment, Drama in ELT, Multimedia, Materials Design, and Qualitative Research methods. In addition to his 20 years in Korea, Dr. Finch has worked in Hong Kong as a testing consultant and has authored various books, international articles, EFL programs and textbooks, and English discussion books. He was visiting research fellow at the Graduate School of Education (TESOL), Bristol University, UK, during his sabbatical year, and his Ph.D. (Manchester University, UK) was on language program assessment. Dr. Finch loves Baduk, hiking, and Cheonggukjang.

Editor: Dr. Heebon Park-Finch is Assistant Professor in the College of Liberal Education of Keimyung University. She has a Ph.D. in Modern British Drama at Bristol University, UK, and a Ph.D. in English Literature at Kyungpook National University. Dr. Park-Finch has written English TV program scripts for Daegu MBC and has worked as International Coordinator and Official Interpreter for the Gyeongju World Culture EXPO Organizing Committee.

MP3 Recording: Michelle Adkisson, Graham Beals, Dr. Dieter Knowle, James Kim, Marc Lapointe, Jeroen Root, Forrest Smith.

초급교양영어

Freshman English 1 - Second Edition (revised)

First published 22 February 2012
Second edition 11 February 2013
Second edition (revised) 20 December 2013

Published by
Kyungpook National University Press

Address | 80 Daehak-ro, Buk-gu, Daegu, Korea
Tel | (+82) 53-950-6741~3 Fax | (+82) 53-953-4692
E-mail | press@knu.ac.kr Website | www.knupress.com

ISBN 978-89-7180-361-5 13740

Foreword

Welcome to the second edition of ***Freshman English, Book 1***. This book offers an integrated, learner-centered, task-based approach to the development of practical English skills. In doing this, it focuses on personal discovery and recognizes language learners as individuals, with their own multiple intelligences. It also encourages the social skills of teamwork, collaboration, negotiation, and responsibility, developing the whole person through informative, challenging, and motivating speaking and writing activities.

Learning a foreign language is one of the most complex activities we perform in our lives, involving logical thinking, emotional management, collaboration, diligence, and responsibility, as well as communication, interaction, and presentation skills. As we discover how to perform various functions in the new language (creating, classifying, comparing, ordering, solving, suggesting, agreeing, choosing, deciding, predicting, and planning), we acquire these skills in different ways and at different speeds, according to our learning styles. Therefore, it is important that we learn *how to learn* as well as *what to learn*, so that we can continue learning for life.

For this reason, every Unit in this book aims to develop problem-solving, critical thinking (description, interpretation, ordering, relating), application (solving, changing, choosing), analysis (deduction, inference, classification), synthesis (creativity, curiosity, imagination, invention), and evaluation (judgment, assessment).

Curiosity is especially important when learning a language, and it is promoted here by encouraging learners to investigate, explore, discover, and share their ideas, using riddles, puzzles, surveys, games, mind-maps, brainstorming, role-plays and quotations from famous people. Not only are thinking skills developed in this way, but learners also become more confident, motivated and independent as their abilities are stretched.

When we have the thinking tools to analyze issues, discuss the causes and effects, and suggest solutions, we can become effective users of the language. ***Freshman English, Book 1*** therefore provides learners with input language, conversation gambits, vocabulary, and guidance about writing form, style and content, in addition to opportunities for practice (output and performance), organization (portfolio), self/peer-assessment, and feedback.

To conclude, I would like to express my thanks and appreciation to the university executive staff who made this program possible, the KNU press staff for their active support, and all the teachers on the Freshman English program who offered their invaluable feedback on the first edition and thereby helped this book to grow into its present form.

Andrew Finch
December 2013

How to use this book

Freshman English 1 has an external structure and an internal structure, both of which place the individual learner at the center, encouraging personal investigation and discovery. The focus gradually becomes wider during the book, developing practical English skills within an ever-expanding context.

External structure:

- **Personal section** (▸Units 1-4). This section helps the individual learner to examine his/her identity, self-esteem, hopes, dreams, ideas, values and learning styles
- **Local section** (▸Units 5-6). The scope is widened to the close surroundings: family, friends, school, music, hobbies, and fashion.
- **General section** (▸Units 7-8). The path of discovery expands to culture, art, people, tourism, nutrition, and history.
- **Global section** (▸Units 9-10). We now look at Spaceship Earth, with its global and human issues such as technology, climate change, alternative energy, and natural resources.
- **Presentation section** (▸Unit 11). This section builds on everything that has been learned so far, offering an opportunity to acquire, develop and rehearse presentation skills.
- **Resources section** (▸Word Bank). The final section contains useful vocabulary, discussion phrases, transition words, a marking code and paragraph checklist, answers to the puzzles that appear in the Units, and an English-Korean glossary of key words.

Internal structure:

The internal structure of each Unit follows a similar path, proceeding from individual work to pairwork and groupwork, before moving on to individual writing and peer-feedback. Each Unit comprises two main sections, which are referred to here as Lesson 1 (speaking) and Lesson 2 (writing), though the integrated nature of the activities means that the four language skills are constantly in use during the process of exploring, finding out, understanding, applying, analyzing, putting it all together, performing, evaluating, and concluding.

Lesson 1 (Speaking):

- **My page** (▸*Generating ideas*, page 1 of each Unit). Learners examine the topic of the Unit by themselves and then in pairs, relating the topic to their own ideas and feelings.
- **Reading and discussing** (▸*Language input*, pages 2-5 of each Unit). Three interesting, informative, and stimulating texts explore the theme of the Unit at different levels of proficiency, offering opportunities to explore new lexis and vocabulary. Post-reading discussions grow from the reading texts.
- **Interacting** (▸*Applying ideas*, page 6 of each Unit). Learners explore the main theme together through surveys, interviews, games, puzzles, questionnaires, role-plays and other interactive tasks, prior to learning how to express related ideas in writing.

Lesson 2 (writing):

- ○ **Writing workshop** (▸*Focus on form*, page 7 of each Unit). Sentence writing skills are developed and practiced through a focus on the mechanics of writing (capitalization, punctuation, apostrophes, personal pronouns, non-count nouns, spelling, prepositions, articles, consistency, and word order).
- ○ **Writing skills** (▸*Exposure and analysis*, pages 8-9 of each Unit). Paragraph writing skills are developed through a focus on paragraph format, paragraph types, cohesive devices (transition words and phrases), and process writing (planning, writing, editing, and revising).
- ○ **Writing practice** (▸*Discussion and output*, page 10 of each Unit). Learners brainstorm, outline, and organize their thoughts before writing the first draft of their paragraph. Classmates edit this draft in class and give peer-feedback. (In Unit 1, the first draft is written on page 11 and is self-edited.)
- ○ **Writing assignment** (▸*Revision and organization*, page 11 of each Unit). Each learner revises his/her first draft and produces a second draft (homework), based on the peer-feedback received in class. This is then placed in the portfolio pocket, in the back cover of the book. Instructors give feedback on three occasions (see page 176), after which each learner writes a final draft and puts this in the portfolio pocket.
- ○ **Review corner** (▸*Reflection*, page 12 of each Unit). Self-assessment and review activities encourage learners to reflect on what they have learned and to prepare for the next Unit.

Web site:

Freshman English 1 has its own Internet web site, designed to supplement and reinforce each Unit. The site can be found at: http://www.finchpark.com/KNUFLE/. Students and teachers are encouraged to visit this site regularly and to browse the links:

- **Reference sites** (online dictionaries, encyclopedias, thesauruses, etc.)
- **Reading** (more reading passages on the theme of the Unit)
- **Writing** (information, exercises and samples of paragraph types and grammar)
- **Listening** (online listening activities
- **Viewing** (related videos)
- **Games and puzzles** (activities for developing curiosity, creativity and thinking skills)
- **Links for teachers** (learning and teaching resources relevant to the content of each Unit)

Audio files:

Students can listen to all the reading passages and sample paragraphs (MP3 free downloads) at http://www.knupress.com.

Contents: Lesson 1

Contents: Lesson 2

UNIT 1 This is me.

My page My profile

Think about yourself and complete these sentences.

1. I am a person who ....
2. I would like to be ....
3. I am happiest when ....
4. One thing I can do well is ....
5. One thing I like about myself is ....
6. My favorite pastime is ....
7. Right now, I feel ....
8. In ten years I ....
9. One of my strongest points is ....
10. If I could have a wish come true, I'd wish for ....
11. I like people who ....
12. The person I admire most is ....
13. A good friend is someone who ....
14. A good student is someone who ....
15. In this course, I would like to ....

Ask a classmate about his/her profile. What kind of person are you?
Compare your abilities and likes. You can swim well, and I can play soccer.

***Today's quotation*:** "The greatest discovery is finding yourself." (Gertrude Moskovitz)

Reading and discussing (step 1)

Track 1

Read this passage, find vocabulary, and then talk about the discussion topics.

Making a Name

Names often have special meanings. Because of this, saints' names and other religious names (Maria, Peter, Sharon) are always popular. Another method of naming is to choose ideas such as faith, truth, wisdom, hope, and brightness.

Some parents choose a fashionable name (a 'fad' name), like that of a famous star. This seems good at first, but when the star is no longer popular, it can sound old-fashioned. A fad name also tells people your age!

If you like your name, you are more likely to feel good about yourself. If you don't, you can change it, along with many famous people who have changed their names. Names are very important. So when you have a newborn baby in your arms, think twice before choosing its name!

You can listen to this passage at http://www.knupress.com.

Vocabulary in context

Are there any words you don't know in this reading passage? Choose two words and write them in the table below. Look in the Glossary (▸pages 151–168) to find their meanings. Make a new sentence for each word and write it in the table.

word	sentence
1	
2	

Discussion topics

1. How are Korean names chosen?

2. Does your name have a special meaning? Tell the others about it.

3. If you have children, what names will you give them? Why?

There are more reading passages at http://www.finchpark.com/KNUFLE/book-1/unit01/read.html.

Reading and discussing (step 2)

Track 2

Read this passage, find vocabulary, and then talk about the discussion topics.

The Family

Aldous Huxley's novel *Brave New World* is ranked 5th in the Modern Library list of the 100 best English language novels of the 20th century. Written in 1931, it is set in the future (London, 2540), at a time when technology has made families unnecessary.

In the novel, the world is a peaceful place, with food and resources for everyone. Nobody is starving or poor. The population is limited to 2 billion (people die at 60) and everyone is happy. Babies are born in Hatcheries, where they are designed for their future jobs. Marriage, natural birth, parenthood, and pregnancy are all things of the past. Nobody has a family, so there are no relatives to mourn them when they die.

This is very different to the world of the 21st century, in which disease, hunger, global warming, and terrorism are common items on the daily News. Huxley's novel therefore raises important questions: 1. What will we sacrifice for a secure life? 2. How important is freedom of thought? 3. Can we live without parents, brothers, sisters, and children?

You can listen to this passage at http://www.knupress.com.

Vocabulary in context

Are there any words you don't know in this reading passage? Choose two words and write them in the table below. Look in the Glossary (▸pages 151–168) to find their meanings. Make a new sentence for each word and write it in the table.

word	sentence
1	
2	

Discussion topics

1. What do you think of the society in Huxley's novel?

2. Talk about the three questions at the end of the passage.

3. Would you like to live in a *Brave New World*? [Yes] Why? [No] Why not?

There are more reading passages at http://www.finchpark.com/KNUFLE/book-1/unit01/read.html.

Reading and discussing (step 3)

Track 3

Read this passage, find vocabulary, and talk about the topics on the next page.

What Do We Need?

What do we need in order to live a happy and healthy life? We need air to breathe, along with food, water, and sleep. But are these enough? Abraham Maslow (1908–1970) wanted to know the answer to this question, so he studied people like Albert Einstein, Jane Addams, Eleanor Roosevelt, and Frederick Douglass, as well as some healthy college students. Then, in 1943, he published his 'hierarchy of needs' pyramid, which you can see on the next page.

The bottom four layers of this pyramid are 'deficiency needs': physiological, safety, friendship and love, and esteem. Physiological needs (layer 1) are the things we need for survival (air, food, water, clothing, and shelter). Without these, the human body cannot continue to function. The need for safety comes next. This layer of the pyramid includes justice, job security, and financial security.

The third layer of human needs is 'social'. We need to feel accepted by other people such as family members, friends, lovers, or teachers. If this need is not met, people can become lonely and even depressed.

The fourth level is 'esteem'. Everyone needs the respect of others, along with self-respect (confidence, independence, and freedom). A lack of self-esteem can cause people to feel weak and inferior.

The final level of the pyramid contains our highest needs. At this level, we try to realize our dreams. This might mean doing well in sport, getting good grades, or expressing ourselves through hobbies. Self-actualization makes us independent and helps us to do things because we love doing them. In order to reach this level, all the lower needs must first be satisfied.

You can listen to this passage at http://www.knupress.com.

Vocabulary in context

Are there any words you don't know in this reading passage? Choose two words and write them in the table below. Look in the Glossary (▸pages 151–168) to find their meanings. Make a new sentence for each word and write it in the table.

word	sentence
1	
2	

There are more reading passages at http://www.finchpark.com/KNUFLE/book-1/unit01/read.html.

Discussion topics

Think about the reading text (▸page 4) and discuss these questions together.

1. What do you think of Maslow's pyramid?
2. What do you know about the people whom Maslow interviewed (paragraph 1)?
3. Why is self-actualization at the top of the pyramid?
4. Where are you on the pyramid?
5. Talk about your dreams. How can you realize them?

Where do you think these words fit in the pyramid?

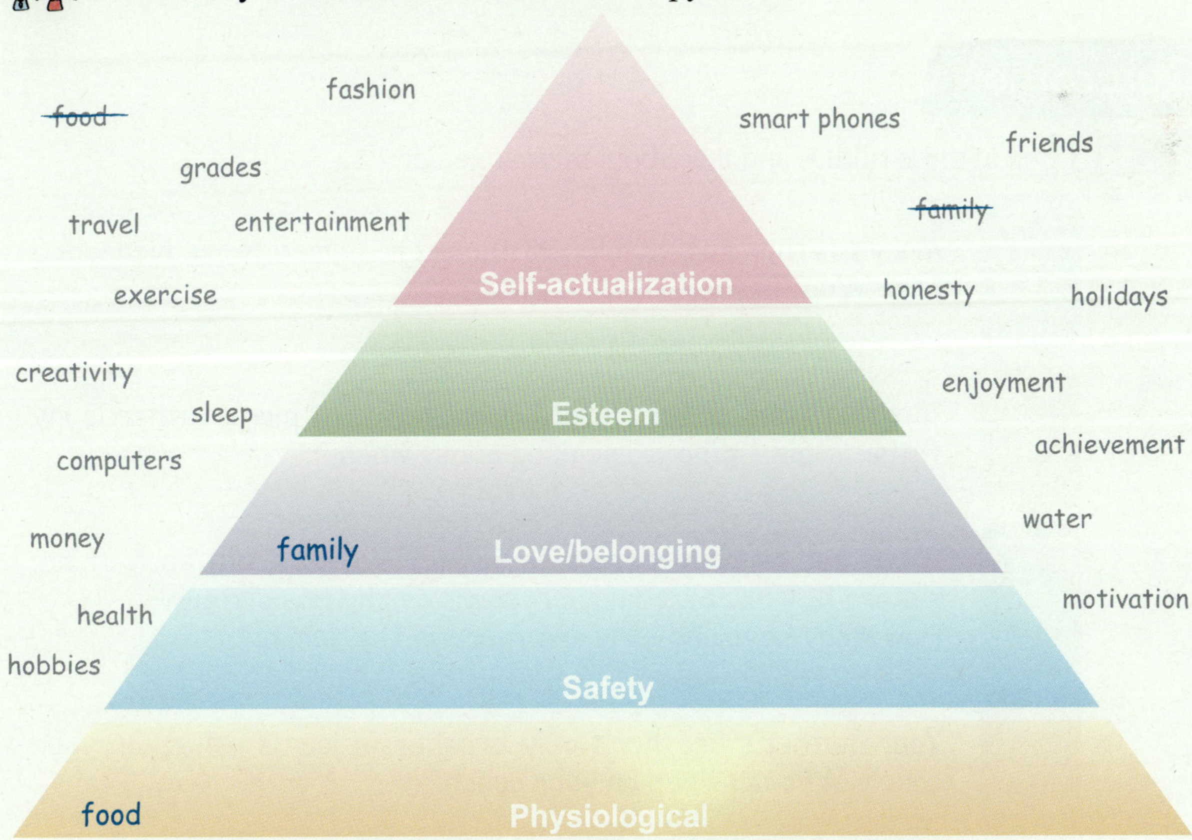

There are lots of helpful discussion phrases in the **Word Bank**, on pages 144 to 150. Check them out whenever you have a discussion activity.

Interacting *Our identities*

Ask three people about their personal profiles (▸page 1).
Write the information in the table below. Does anyone have the same answers as you?

questions / names			
What kind of person are you?			
What would you like to be?			
When are you happiest?			
What do you like about yourself?			
What is your favorite pastime?			
How do you feel now?			
What is your strongest point?			
What would you wish for?			
Whom do you admire most?			
What is a good friend?			
What do you want from this course?			

Quiz corner

Look at these riddles and talk about them together.

1. Mary's father has 4 children; three are named Nana, Nene, and Nini. What is the 4th child's name?

2. "Brothers and sisters have I none, but that man's father is my father's son." Who is speaking about whom?

3. A boy has as many sisters as he has brothers, but each of his sisters has twice as many brothers as she has sisters.
How many boys and girls are there in the family?

4. Your mother's brother's only brother-in-law is asleep on your couch. Who is asleep on your couch?

The solutions are in the **Answer Section** at the back of the book.
There are more quizzes on the Unit 1 website ("Games & Puzzles").

Writing workshop *The paragraph*

Here is some information about paragraphs.

A paragraph is a series of sentences with the same topic or central idea. There are three parts to a paragraph:

1. **Topic sentence:** This is usually the first sentence. It expresses the main idea of the paragraph.
2. **Supporting sentences:** These develop the idea of the topic sentence.
3. **Concluding sentence:** This is a final statement about the main idea.

A well-written paragraph has four characteristics:

1. **Unity:** The paragraph should discuss only one idea.
2. **Completeness:** There are enough supporting sentences to explain the topic.
3. **Cohesion:** There is a smooth, continuous flow of ideas. Cohesion is helped by the use of personal pronouns (I, we, you, she, he, it, they), demonstrative pronouns (this, that, these, those), articles (a, an, the), synonyms, and transitions (first, next, then, ...).
4. **Continuity:** Each sentence grows out of the previous one and leads naturally into the next.

Draw lines from the circled words to the parts of the paragraph that they refer to.

Topic sentence | Supporting sentence 1 | Supporting sentence 2

Track 4

The sandwich has an interesting history. This food was named after John Montagu (1718-1792), 4th Earl of Sandwich, England, who ordered his servant to bring him meat between two pieces of bread when he was playing cards. Since then, the sandwich has usually consisted of two slices of bread with fillings between them. By the early 20th century, it was popular in the United States. Furthermore, it quickly became America's most popular meal. The sandwich is now a popular type of food around the world.

You can listen to this passage at http://www.knupress.com.

Supporting sentence 3 | Supporting sentence 4 | Concluding sentence | articles

Personal pronouns | Demonstrative pronouns | Transitions

You can find more information about paragraphs on the "Writing" website for this Unit: http://www.finchpark.com/KNUFLE/book-1/unit01/writing.html.

Writing skills *Writing an e-mail*

An e-mail should contain 5 parts:

1. **Subject** A clear, short, summary of the content of the message
2. **Greeting** The title (Mr., Mrs., Ms., Dr.) and the name of the other person
3. **Body** The content of the message
4. **Closing** A positive ending to the message
5. **Signature** The writer's name, along with contact information

Highlight, underline, or circle the five parts in this sample e-mail:

To: J.Brown@eflteach.com

Subject: My introduction

Attach a file | Receipt On Read : ☐ | Receipt On Delivery : ☐

Cc | Bcc | Signature | Addresses | Save Draft | Send | Check Spelling

Dear Ms. Brown,

This is my introduction. My name is Moon Seok-gi (Steven) and I was born in Busan, where I went to elementary school. Then we moved to Daegu and I went to middle school and high school there, before coming to university. There are four people in my family. My father has his own business and my mother looks after the house. She also takes care of my sister, who goes to middle school. When I have spare time I like to listen to music and read books. I also like to walk to school for exercise. Health is most important in my opinion. I want to be an engineer after I graduate, so I need to study hard and I need to learn English.

I look forward to taking your class.

Best wishes,

Steven Moon

Mobile: (012) 345-6789

Analyze the main paragraph in this e-mail using the checklist below.

- ☐ *Where is the topic sentence of the paragraph? Underline it.*
- ☐ *Where is the concluding sentence? Underline it.*
- ☐ *Does the paragraph discuss only one idea? (Unity)*
- ☐ *Is there a smooth, continuous flow of ideas? (Cohesion)*
- ☐ *Does each sentence lead naturally into the next one? (Continuity)*

Writing skills *Writing an e-mail*

Now look at this e-mail. Talk about it together. How can it be improved?

To: J.Brown@eflteach.com

Subject: Hi teacher! :)

Attach a file | Receipt On Read : ☐ | Receipt On Delivery : ☐

Cc | Bcc | Signature | Addresses | Save Draft | Send | Check Spelling

Hey, teacher,

how's it going? i'm Kim Ji-seok. call me Dave.
I'M SO HAPPY TO BE IN YOUR CLASS. ^^
how long ru in Korea? where did you come from?
how old ru? what do you think Korea?
i'm born in Seoul. My family is 4 people. father works in the bank and mother works supermrket. my sister studies high school.
i like music. movies, and hiking. my sport favorite is basketball. i will be businessman. Haha.
btw, I hope this homework is ok. i did my best. ㅠㅠ
cu next class ... bfn

Rewrite the e-mail. Check the guidelines on pages 7 and 8.

To

Subject

Attach a file | Receipt On Read : ☐ | Receipt On Delivery : ☐

Cc | Bcc | Signature | Addresses | Save Draft | Send | Check Spelling

You can see a sample answer in the **Word Bank**, on page 142.

Writing practice *Formal and informal e-mail language*

E–mails use formal or informal language, depending on the situation.

Part 1: Subject

Formal		Informal	
My introduction	My family	Some questions	Congratulations!
My resumé	Job application	Good news	What's new?
Greetings from Korea	Letter of reference	How about Friday?	Lunch on Monday

Part 2: Greeting

Formal		Informal	
Dear Classmates,	Dear Ms. Lee,	Hi!	Hello,
Dear Professor Kim,	Dear Dr. Smith,	Hi there!	Dear Jo,
Dear Mr. Jones,	Dear Sir/Madam,	Kevin, (name only)	

Part 3: Body

Formal	Informal
Thank you for your e-mail.	Thanks for the e-mail.
Regarding ...	Re ...
I would be grateful if ...	Please could you ...
Please accept my apologies for ...	I'm sorry for ...
However, ... / In addition, ... / Therefore, ...	But, ... / Also, ... / So, ...
... as soon as possible.	... asap
Please find my assignment attached.	Assignment attached.
I look forward to meeting you next week.	See you next week.
I look forward to hearing from you.	Hear from you soon.
Please do not hesitate to contact me.	Let me know if you need more.

Part 4: Closing

Formal		Informal	
Best regards,	Yours sincerely,	All the best,	Good luck!
Best wishes,	Yours truly,	Bye for now,	Take care,
Respectfully yours,	Many thanks,	Until next time,	Write soon.
Yours faithfully,		Have a great weekend.	Your friend,

Discussion

1. When do you think you should use formal language in e-mails?

2. When do you think you should use informal language in e-mails?

There is more information about formal and informal language on the "Writing" site for this Unit: http://www.finchpark.com/KNUFLE/book-1/unit01/writing.html.

Writing assignment *Writing an e-mail to the teacher*

Here are some tips for writing e-mails.

1. Write a meaningful subject – short and clear.
2. Start the message with a greeting.
3. Identify yourself clearly.
4. Be brief and to the point.
5. Use short, simple sentences.
6. Check for formal and informal language.
7. Avoid abbreviations and emoticons.
8. Re-read, review and edit the e-mail before sending.
9. Include your name at the end of the message.
10. End the message politely.

Write an e-mail to your teacher. Introduce yourself and tell him/her what you want to learn in this class. Look at the guidelines on pages 7, 8, and 10, and check the tips above.

To

Subject

Attach a file | Receipt On Read : ☐ | Receipt On Delivery : ☐

Cc | Bcc | Signature | Addresses | Save Draft | Send | Check Spelling

Review corner *Self-assessment and Self-study*

How did you do in this Unit? Fill in this self-assessment sheet.

Name: Date:

1. How were your reading skills (▸pages 2, 3, and 4)?

2. How were your discussion skills (▸pages 2, 3, 5, 6, and 10)?

3. How was your written assignment (▸page 11)?

4. What did you do well in this Unit?

5. What do you need to improve?

Review what you have done in this Unit and prepare for the next Unit.

http://www.finchpark.com/KNUFLE/book-1/index.html

- [x] **Review:** Browse the website for Unit 1.
- [ ] **Preview:** Browse the website for Unit 2.
- [ ] **Prepare:** Look at the activities in Unit 2.
- [ ] **Organize:** Cut out this page. Put it in the portfolio pocket at the back of the book.

UNIT 2 My world

My page My introduction

Think of some good events that have happened to you.
Draw (or attach photos of) three of the best events below.

Talk to a classmate about the good things that have happened to him/her.
What are your best events? When did they happen?

> ***Today's quotation*:** "Try not to become a man of success but rather try to become a man of value." (Albert Einstein)

Reading and discussing (step 1)

Track 5

Read this passage, find vocabulary, and then talk about the discussion topics.

Happiness Within

What is happiness? How is it different from wealth, honor, health or friendship? According to Aristotle, happiness is the main thing that humans look for in their lives. The American Declaration of Independence (1776) states that the pursuit of happiness is a human right.

Here is a list of tips for happiness:

1. **Laugh.**
2. **Exercise.**
3. **Have a goal.**
4. **Treat yourself.**
5. **Do something you love.**
6. **Count your blessings.**
7. **Notice small things.**
8. **Follow your passions.**
9. **Show little acts of kindness.**
10. **Learn something new.**

Vocabulary in context

Choose two unfamiliar words and write them in the table. Find their meanings in the Glossary (▸pages 151–168). Make a sentence for each word and write it in the table.

word	sentence
1	
2	

Discussion topics

1. What makes you happy?
2. Why is happiness important?
3. What are your tips for happiness? Talk about them.

There are more reading passages at http://www.finchpark.com/KNUFLE/book-1/unit02/read.html.

Reading and discussing (step 2)

Track 6

Read this passage, find vocabulary, and then talk about the discussion topics.

Values

Personal values are made up of moral, political, religious, and social values. They help us to decide what is right and wrong. Albert Einstein (1879–1955) thought values were very important. Here are some of his life lessons and his comments about them:

1. Work towards a goal.
2. Allow yourself to make mistakes. — *Anyone who has never made a mistake has never tried anything new.*
3. Keep your mind alert by being curious.
4. Focus on what you are doing with your whole strength and soul.
5. Realize that what you do results in consequences. — *I shall never believe that God plays dice with the world.*
6. Think new.
7. Don't give up. — *It's not that I'm smart. I just stay with problems longer.*
8. Create value.
9. Imagine. — *Imagination is more important than knowledge.*
10. Be in the present. — *I never think of the future. It comes soon enough.*

Vocabulary in context

Choose two unfamiliar words and write them in the table. Find their meanings in the Glossary (▸pages 151–168). Make a sentence for each word and write it in the table.

word	sentence
1	
2	

Discussion topics

1. Why do we need values?
2. Do you agree with Einstein's life lessons? [Yes] Why? [No] Why not?
3. What are the most important values in your life? Talk about them.

There are more reading passages at http://www.finchpark.com/KNUFLE/book-1/unit02/read.html.

Reading and discussing (step 3)

Track 7

Read this passage, find vocabulary, and talk about the topics on the next page.

Beautiful Dreamer

When we dream about our future, or 'wish upon a star', we usually think of a good job, a loving family, success, and happiness. But what if we only had one year to live? How would our dreams be different? What would we want to do in that year? *The Bucket List* (2007) is a movie that asks this question. In the film, two terminally ill men make a list of all the things they want to do before they kick the bucket, and then they do them! As a result, they discover an unusual but wonderful friendship.

You're never too young or too old to make a bucket list, so how about making a list of 10 things you want to do in this life? This will help you to find out what really matters to you. You don't have to wait forever to achieve your dreams.

Another way to celebrate being alive is to make a list of small or unusual things that you'd love to do. If you do one of them every day, you will learn how to seize the moment (*carpe diem*) and enjoy every day of your life. Here are some examples:

- ✓ Fly a kite.
- ✓ Read a poem.
- ✓ Clean your room.
- ✓ Watch the sunrise.
- ✓ Sing in the shower.
- ✓ Go for a walk on campus.
- ✓ Cook a meal for your parents.
- ✓ Help an old lady carry her bags.
- ✓ Give your seat on the bus to someone who looks tired.

We should never be afraid to dream: "Dream what you want to dream, go where you want to go, be what you want to be; you have only one life and one chance to do all the things you want to do." (Anonymous)

Vocabulary in context

Choose three unfamiliar words from this passage and write them below. Look in the Glossary (▸pages 151–168) for their meanings. Make a new sentence for each word.

word	sentence
1	
2	
3	

There are more reading passages at http://www.finchpark.com/KNUFLE/book-1/unit02/read.html.

Discussion topics

Think about the reading text (▸page 16) and discuss these questions together.

1. Have you ever been impressed by a movie? Why was it impressive?

2. Have you ever watched the sunrise? [Yes] How was it? [No] Why not?

3. What would you like to add to the list on page 16?

4. Do you have a dream? [Yes] Talk about it. [No] Why not?

5. How can we make our dreams come true?

Talk to each other about your dreams and then make your own bucket list.

1. ____________________
2. ____________________
3. ____________________
4. ____________________
5. ____________________
6. ____________________
7. ____________________
8. ____________________
9. ____________________
10. ____________________

My bucket list

Interacting *Time capsule*

Imagine that you are going to make a time capsule. It will be opened 100 years later. What will you put in the time capsule?

- Think of the things you use every day.
- Think of the things that are important to you.
- Write their names or draw them in the time capsule, below.

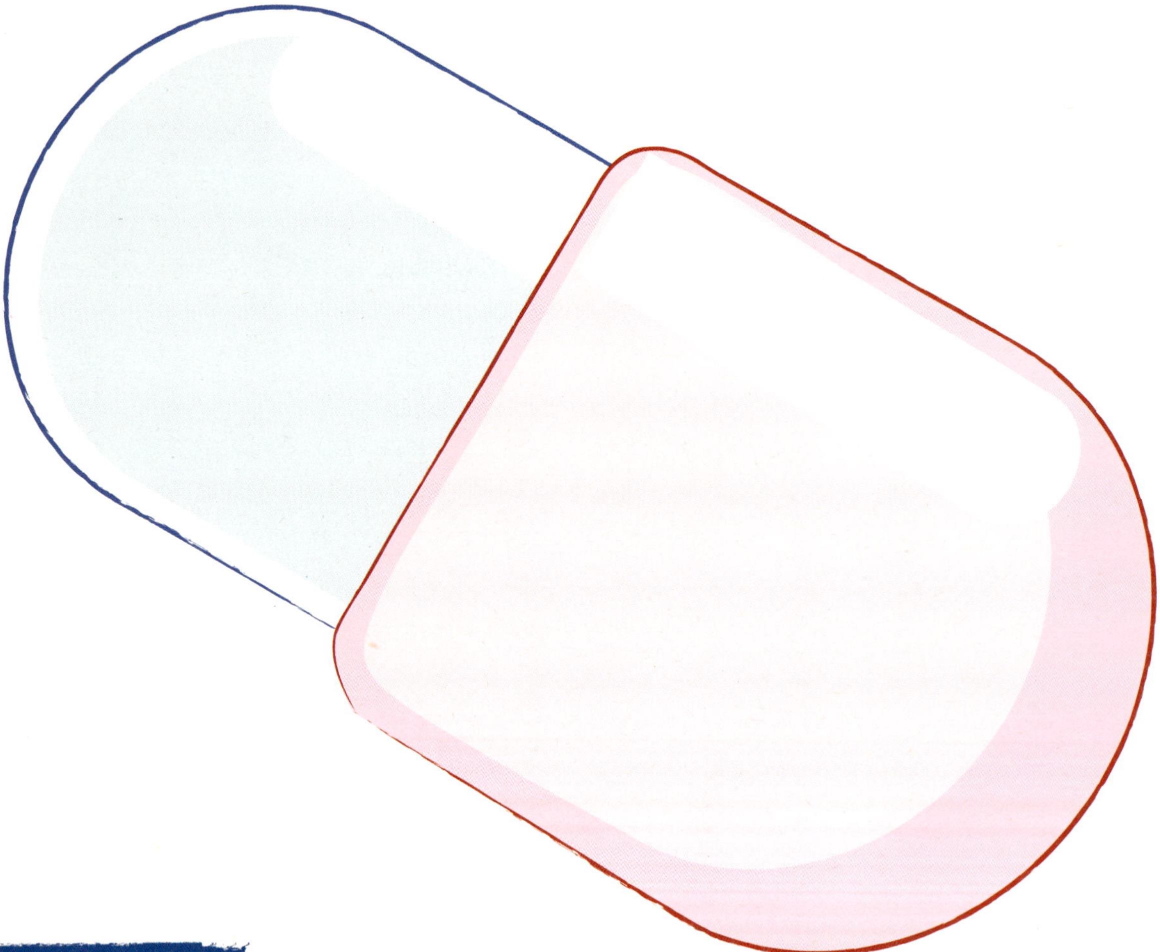

Quiz corner

Discuss these riddles and try to find solutions.

What building has the most stories? ______________________

What city has no people? ______________________

What kind of clothes does a house wear? ______________________

What gets wetter as it dries? ______________________

The solutions to these riddles are in the **Answer Section** at the back of the book.

Writing workshop Capitals

What is wrong with these sentences? Talk about them together and edit them, using the "**C**" code for "Capitals" (▸page 141).

1. hello. my name is charles. i come from tunisia.
2. dr. foster went to washington last tuesday.
3. every time i visit seoul i go to the kimchi museum.
4. my favorite movie is called the matrix. keanu reeves is the main star.
5. every sentence starts with a capital letter. proper nouns have capitals too.

The answers are in the **Answer Section** at the back of the book (▸page 169).
More capitalization activities: http://www.finchpark.com/KNUFLE/book-1/unit02/writing.html.

Writing skills The listing paragraph

Track 8

Here is a listing paragraph. It contains five happiness tips from page 14.

Happiness

There are many ways we can become happier in our lives. For example, laughing helps us to feel good. In addition, exercise is good for the body and helps to get oxygen into the lungs. Then again, having a goal gives us something to focus on. It is also a good idea to treat ourselves from time to time and to do something we love doing. Of course, there are many more ways to become happier, but these are some simple ideas that we can begin with.

- ☐ Can you find the 5 tips? Circle them.
- ☐ Highlight the transition words (▸page 20).
- ☐ Where is the topic sentence? Underline it.
- ☐ Where is the conclusion sentence? Underline it.

Writing skills *The listing paragraph*

The paragraph on page 19 shows how lists become paragraphs.

1. The main idea becomes the **topic sentence**.
2. The list items become **supporting sentences**.
3. The sentences are linked with **transition words**.
4. A **concluding** sentence is added.

Here are some transition words. There are more in the Word Bank, on page 150 ("Sequencing").

First,	In addition,	For example,	However,	For this reason,
Then,	Similarly,	For instance,	On the one hand,	Therefore,
Next,	Furthermore,	In particular,	On the other hand,	As a result,
Finally,	In the same way,	In fact,	In contrast,	In conclusion,

Choose three items from the lists on pages 14, 15, or 16. Make notes for a listing paragraph with the three items.

1. Title ....
2. Topic sentence ....
3. Transition word(s) ....
4. Supporting sentence 1 ....
5. Transition word(s) ....
6. Supporting sentence 2 ....
7. Transition word(s) ....
8. Supporting sentence 3 ....
9. Transition word(s) ....
10. Conclusion sentence ....

There are links about listing paragraphs on the website for this Unit:
http://www.finchpark.com/KNUFLE/book-1/unit02/writing.html.

Writing skills *Brainstorming*

Before we start writing a paragraph, we need to find ideas. Brainstorming is a great way of doing this. We simply write down all the ideas as we think of them. Any ideas are OK.

Let's do some brainstorming now and prepare for the writing practice on page 22 and the assignment on page 23.

Choose one of these topics for a listing paragraph:

1. My time capsule
2. My values
3. My bucket list
4. ______________________(your own topic)

Now brainstorm your topic together. Write any ideas that come to you.

Have you checked out the videos on the Unit 2 website ("Viewing")?

Writing practice *Making and editing a listing paragraph*

Choose four items from the brainstorming you did on page 21.
Write your items here:

1. ______________________ 3. ______________________

2. ______________________ 4. ______________________

Now make a listing paragraph with these four items. Indent the 1st line by 3–5 spaces.

Draft 1

____

Peer-editing

Exchange books with a classmate. Edit his/her first draft. Use the Paragraph Checklist below. Return the book to your classmate and talk about your first drafts together.

Paragraph Checklist	✓
Capital letters (C – pages 19 and 141)	☐
Title	☐
Topic sentence	☐
Concluding sentence	☐

Writing assignment Rewriting: Final draft

On page 22, a classmate edited your first draft. Now rewrite your listing paragraph, based on this editing and on your own ideas.

Name: ____________________ Final draft

My notes

Review corner Self-assessment: Personal qualities

Look at the "Personal qualities" words on page 140. Choose words that describe your health, values, emotions and feelings, beliefs and needs. Write a sentence about each quality.

Words and sentences that describe me	
Health	
Values	
Emotions and feelings	
Beliefs	
Needs	

Review what you have done in this Unit and prepare for the next Unit.

My To Do List!

- [ ] **1. Review:** Browse the website for Unit 2.
- [ ] **2. Preview:** Browse the website for Unit 3.
- [ ] **3. Prepare:** Look at the activities in Unit 3.
- [ ] **4. Organize:** Cut out this page. Put it in the portfolio pocket.

http://www.finchpark.com/KNUFLE/book-1/

UNIT 3 My feelings

My page Emotions

Are you an emotional person? Do you show your feelings?
Write about your emotions below:

Q 1: What makes you happy?

Q 2: What makes you sad?

Q 3: What makes you excited?

Q 4: What makes you worried?

Q 5: What makes you proud?

Q 6: What makes you embarrassed?

Q 7: What makes you feel grateful?

Q 8: What makes you feel peaceful?

Talk to a classmate about your feelings. I am happy when ...
Ask about his/her feelings. Why do you feel that way?

Today's quotation: "The best and most beautiful things in the world cannot be seen or touched, but are felt in the heart." (Helen Keller)

Reading and discussing (step 1)

Track 9

Read this passage, find vocabulary, and then talk about the discussion topics.

Animal Feelings

Do animals have feelings? Are they ever happy, sad, or angry? Do they have memories? Do they think? Pet lovers have always answered 'Yes' to these questions and scientists are beginning to agree with them. In fact, as long ago as 1872, Charles Darwin wrote a book called *The Expression of the Emotions in Man and Animals*. In this book, which was one of the first to contain photographs, Darwin says that humans and animals have similar minds.

The problem is that we can't talk with animals and ask them how they feel. All we can do is watch their actions. Most people agree that animals feel pain and fear, since these are needed for survival. But some say there is no proof that animals have feelings. What do you think?

Vocabulary in context

Choose two unfamiliar words and write them in the table. Find the meanings in the Glossary (▸pages 151–168). Make a sentence for each word and write it in the table.

word	sentence
1	
2	

Discussion topics

1. Do you think animals have feelings? Explain your opinion.

2. Why do you think people have pets?

3. Is it OK to use animals for scientific experiments? [Yes] Why? [No] Why not?

There are more reading passages at http://www.finchpark.com/KNUFLE/book-1/unit03/read.html.

Reading and discussing (step 2)

Track 10

Read this passage, find vocabulary, and then talk about the discussion topics.

Positive or Negative?

Emotions can be positive and negative. Positive emotions help us to broaden our minds and express our feelings. Negative emotions help us to avoid danger, but they can make us do things we regret. However, they are all part of our identity. We need to accept our emotions and learn how to manage them. Here are some useful tips:

1. **Watch your emotions.** Ask yourself: "How am I feeling right now?"
2. **Learn how to be positive.** Don't let negative ideas gain control.
3. **Give yourself a break.** Don't punish yourself for not being perfect.
4. **Look at problems as challenges.** Every cloud has a silver lining.
5. **You can't please everyone.** Don't try too hard to be loved.
6. **Don't blame fate.** Your life is what you make it.
7. **Learn from your mistakes.** Don't give up.
8. **Be positive.** Look on the bright side.
9. **Trust yourself.** Believe in yourself.
10. **Forgive yourself.** Be kind to yourself.

Vocabulary in context

Choose two unfamiliar words and write them in the table. Find their meanings in the Glossary (▸pages 151–168). Make a sentence for each word and write it in the table.

word	sentence
1	
2	

Discussion topics

1. Do you look on the bright side of life? [Yes] Why? [No] Why not?

2. Do you believe in yourself? Please explain.

3. How can we be more positive in our lives?

There are more reading passages at http://www.finchpark.com/KNUFLE/book-1/unit03/read.html.

Reading and discussing (step 3)

Track 11

Read this passage, find vocabulary, and talk about the topics on the next page.

Avoiding Burnout

Some types of stress can be good for us and others can cause major health problems. We need to understand the different types in order to learn how to deal with them and live a healthy life. There are four major types of stress:

1. **Eustress** is a helpful type of stress. It prepares the muscles, heart, and mind for what is about to happen. Athletes often experience this before they play a big game or enter a big competition.
2. **Distress** is a negative type of stress. It occurs when the normal routine is upset. There are two types of distress: acute stress and chronic stress.
   - **Acute stress** comes when we suddenly change a routine. It is the body's way of checking that everything is OK.
   - **Chronic stress** affects people who are always changing their routine, like shift workers in factories or business people who do a lot of traveling.
3. **Hyperstress** is a negative type of stress. It appears when a person has too much work on a regular basis. This can cause emotional and physical harm as well as exhaustion.
4. **Hypostress** is a lack of stress. People who are always bored, doing the same job every day, can suffer from hypostress.

Continuous stress can lead to burnout, and some companies are taking this problem seriously. They are making de-stressed recreational areas where the staff can relax and play pool, basketball, or table tennis. They hope that this will increase not only the employees' health, but also their efficiency, resulting in more income for the company.

Vocabulary in context

Choose three unfamiliar words from this passage and write them below. Look in the Glossary (▸pages 151–168) for their meanings. Write a new sentence for each word.

word	sentence
1	
2	
3	

There are more reading passages at http://www.finchpark.com/KNUFLE/book-1/unit03/read.html.

Discussion topics

Think about the reading text (▸page 28) and discuss these questions together. Here are some "Giving an opinion" phrases to help you (▸page 148).

I think …	My view is ...	In my opinion,	Personally speaking,
In my view,	To my mind …	I believe that ...	From my point of view,
As I see it, ...	It seems to me,		

1. How did you feel when you read the text? Why?

2. What sorts of stress do you experience? Talk about your stress.

3. What do you do to relieve stress?

4. Is it better to be an optimist or a pessimist? Explain your opinion.

Look at the negative thinking types below and talk to a classmate about them: Do you ever think like this?

1 Black & White thinking
Everything is either very good or very bad. You blame yourself if you are not perfect.

2 Ignoring the positive
You don't believe people who praise you, but you completely believe people who criticize you.

3 Emotional reasoning
You rely on your negative emotions: "I feel unhappy, so there must be something wrong."

4 Overgeneralization
One negative event becomes all-important. "I failed the driving test yesterday. I'll never drive a car."

5 Fortune teller
You always think of bad results. Then if something bad happens, you tell yourself that you knew it was going to happen.

6 'Should' statements
You keep telling yourself you 'should', 'must' or 'ought to' do something. This only makes you feel guilty.

Interacting Family feelings

Make a group role-play about family relationships.

1. Choose a role card (Father, Mother, Daughter, or Son).
2. Think about your role and make notes at the bottom of the page.
3. Perform the role-play together. (You can change the situation if you wish.)

Role card: Father

Your son is getting poor grades at school. You've told him that he must study hard and get into a good university. You followed your parents' wishes and became a doctor. Your son must do the same.

Role-card: Mother

Your son isn't happy at school. He wants to be a singer. You know that his father will never agree to this. You love your son and you love your husband. You want them both to agree.

Role-card: Daughter

Your brother thinks about singing all the time. He won't listen to his teachers or his father. He never goes out with his friends. You want him to be happy, but you don't know how to help him.

Role-card: Son

Music is everything for you. You want to be a professional singer. You know your parents don't agree and you want to please them, but you don't want to be a doctor. If only they would understand!

My Notes

There are many phrases for your role-play in the **Word Bank**. ▸Page 144: Adding a point, Advantages, Advice; ▸Page 145: Agreement, Approval, Argument; ▸Page 147: Comprehension, Concession; ▸Page 148: Giving an opinion; ▸Page 149: Giving reasons; ▸Page 150: Suggesting, Summarizing, Wants, needs and wishes.

Writing workshop — Punctuation and Capitalization

Can you match these punctuation signs with their names?

colon   comma   asterisk   semi-colon   question mark   quotation marks

“ ”   .   ,   !   ;   :   -   ?   ’   ( )   [ ]   *

period   hyphen   apostrophe   parentheses   square brackets   exclamation mark

The correct use of punctuation and capitalization makes your writing clear and easy to understand. Discuss the following sentences and rewrite them:

1. michael is a student in ucla

2. is central park in the usa

3. mr smith said come here at once

4. the capital of england is london isnt it

5. a man chooses a slave obeys

6. excuse me wheres the station

7. im visiting these places paris france berlin germany and rome italy

Quiz corner

Correct the punctuation and then solve this puzzle.

you are driving a bus four people get on and three people get off then eight people get on and ten people get off then six people get on and two more people get off what color are the bus drivers eyes

All the answers for this page are in the **Answer Section** at the back of the book

There are more punctuation activities on the Unit 3 website: www.finchpark.com/KNUFLE/book-1/unit03/writing.html.

Writing skills *The description paragraph (1)*

Track 12

Description paragraphs are used to write about places, things and people. Here is a sample description paragraph about a person:

My Friend

Let me tell you about my friend. She has shoulder-length, dark-brown, wavy hair, and there is always a smile on her face. My friend likes to look smart, so she often wears a silk scarf round her neck and a green jacket, over a blue blouse. She sometimes wears a gray skirt and black tights, but she is usually to be seen in stylish jeans. As for shoes, she often wears trainers or even sandals. She doesn't follow the latest fashion unless it's comfortable.

Let's play '20 Questions' about people in the class.

One person: Choose someone in the class. Don't tell the others who it is. Answer "Yes" or "No" when the others ask you questions.

Other people: Ask questions. Try to find out who the person is.

Is she tall?
Is she wearing glasses?
Does she have straight hair?
Is he wearing black shoes?
Does he have short hair?
Does she have brown eyes?

Here are some 'people' words that you can use (▸page 139).

Parts of the body

ankle	chest	finger	hand	heel	leg	shoulder	thumb	wrist
arm	elbow	foot	head	knee	neck	stomach	toe	

Parts of the face

cheek	ears	eyelash	eyes	forehead	jaw	mouth	nostril
chin	eyebrow	eyelid	face	hair	lip	nose	tooth

Types of hair

black	braids	brunette	curly	fuzzy	perm	ponytail	straight
blonde	brown	bun	dyed	gray	pigtails	red hair	wavy

Compound adjectives

average-looking	curly-haired	left-handed	quick-tempered	slim-hipped
brown-eyed	easy-going	long-legged	quick-witted	suntanned
broad-shouldered	good-natured	open-minded	self-centered	warm-hearted

More about description paragraphs: http://www.finchpark.com/KNUFLE/book-1/unit03/writing.html.

Writing skills *The description paragraph (2)*

Description paragraphs usually start with the main idea and then describe the details.
Here are some directions that description paragraphs can take:

Subject	Direction	Order of sentences
Person Thing Place	Large to small, small to large	From the whole body to the body parts
	Top to bottom, bottom to top	From the head to the feet (vertically)
	Left to right, right to left	From the left to the right (horizontally)
	Outside to center, center to outside	From the walls to the middle (room)
	North to south, east to west	From one part on a map to another

What direction does the 'person' paragraph on page 32 take?
What direction does the 'place' paragraph below take?

Track 13

Central Park

Central Park in New York is the largest city park in the United States. It is 4 km long and 0.8 km wide and covers 341 hectares. It is bordered by Central Park West, 59th Street, 5th Avenue, and Central Park North. The park contains man-made lakes, walking paths, and natural woods, as well as two ice-rinks. There is a large reservoir near the center, with a running track around it. The Great Lawn, in the center of the park, is perhaps the most famous lawn in the world. All in all, Central Park is a great place to visit.

You are sending a postcard of Central Park to a friend. Describe the scene. Use the 'location words' on page 139.

Check out the listening links on the Unit 3 website ("Listening").

Writing practice *Brainstorming, outlining, first draft*

Choose a topic for your description paragraph, or make your own topic.

1. Someone I admire 2. My dream house 3. A strange object 4. ______________

Brainstorm about your topic and make a mind map of your ideas.

Now write a description paragraph about your topic.

Draft 1

____

____

____

____

____

____

____

____

____

Peer-editing

Exchange books with a classmate. Edit his/her first draft. Look for capitals, punctuation, and paragraph format (▸page 141). Return the book and talk about your first drafts together.

Writing assignment Rewriting and teacher editing

Rewrite your description paragraph, based on your classmate's editing (▸page 34) and on your own ideas. When you have finished, cut out this page and give this second draft to the teacher for editing.

Name: ____________________ Second draft

Teacher's Feedback

When you get your second draft back, write your final draft on the next page.

Writing assignment *Final draft*

Rewrite your paragraph, based on the teacher's feedback. This is your final draft.

Final draft

Review what you have done in this Unit and prepare for the next Unit.

Review	• Browse the website for Unit 3.
Preview	• Browse the website for Unit 4.
Prepare	• Look at the activities in Unit 4.
Organize	• Put this page in the portfolio pocket.

http://www.finchpark.com/KNUFLE/book-1/

UNIT 4 My learning

My page My learning style

What type of learner are you?
Answer the questions below to find out (✓):

	Yes, this is true of me.	This is sometimes true of me.	No, this is not really true of me.
1. I learn best when the teacher tells us everything.			
2. I like to see information on the board or screen.			
3. I like to write things down or take notes in class.			
4. I like to do speaking activities in class.			
5. I need the teacher to explain diagrams and charts.			
6. I enjoy working with my hands or making things.			
7. I am good at making graphs and charts.			
8. I can copy the teacher's pronunciation well.			
9. I remember things by writing them many times.			
10. I can follow directions on maps easily.			
11. I learn best by listening to lectures.			
12. I play with things on the desk when studying.			
13. I learn new words by saying them many times.			
14. I chew gum or eat snacks while I am studying.			
15. I am good at doing puzzles.			
16. I like to hold and touch things when I am learning.			
17. I learn best by reading.			
18. I follow spoken directions better than written ones.			

This activity is based on page 30 of *English Reflections*. A. Finch (2010). KNU Press.

Talk to a classmate. What's your answer to number 1?
Talk about your learning styles. How do you like to learn?

Today's quotation: "Learn from yesterday, live for today, hope for tomorrow." (Albert Einstein)

Reading and discussing (step 1)

Track 14

Read this passage, find vocabulary, and then talk about the discussion topics.

Why is Learning Important?

There are many reasons for learning. Firstly, we are now in the Knowledge Age. This means that we need to be able to find knowledge and use it. Secondly, technology is always changing. Smart technology has changed our lives in a very short time, so it seems that learning new job skills will be necessary in the future. Thirdly, learning can lead to a better quality of life. It helps us make the most of our talents. In conclusion, we all have the ability to learn throughout our lives. As the saying goes, it's never too late to learn.

Vocabulary in context

Choose two or three unfamiliar words and write them in the table. Find the meanings in the Glossary (▸pages 151–168). Write a sentence for each word.

word	sentence
1	
2	
3	

Discussion topics

1. Do you agree with the last sentence of the passage? Why? Why not?

2. What do you think of e-learning? Explain your opinion.

3. Why is it important to learn a foreign language?

There are more reading passages at http://www.finchpark.com/KNUFLE/book-1/unit04/read.html.

Reading and discussing (step 2)

Track 15

Read these proverbs, find vocabulary, and discuss the topics below.

Step by step

Well begun is half done.

Rome wasn't built in a day.

Education is not the filling of a pail but the lighting of a fire.

Mistakes are our teachers; they help us to learn.

There is no royal road to learning.

Practice makes perfect.

You can take a horse to water, but you can't make it drink.

Better late than never!

The man who never made a mistake never made anything.

Learning is a treasure that will follow its owner everywhere.

Teach me and I'll forget. Show me and I'll remember. Involve me and I'll understand.

If you give a man a fish, you feed him for a day. If you teach him how to fish, you feed him for life.

You are never too old to learn.

Vocabulary in context

Choose two or three unfamiliar words and write them in the table. Find the meanings (Glossary ▸pages 151–168). Write a sentence for each word.

word	sentence
1	
2	
3	

Discussion topics

1. Which of the proverbs on this page is most important for you? Why?
2. Do you know any Korean proverbs about learning? Talk about them.
3. What is your motto or favorite proverb? Why did you choose it?

There are more reading passages at http://www.finchpark.com/KNUFLE/book-1/unit04/read.html.

Reading and discussing (step 3)

Track 16

Read this passage, find vocabulary, and talk about the topics on the next page.

Learning for Life

What is education? What is learning? Why do we go to school? These questions are extremely important in these days of Information Technology (IT), Artificial Intelligence (AI), and e-learning. Educators are now talking about a Learning Revolution. They say 21st century schools should teach students how to learn, since many of the jobs they will do in the future haven't been invented yet. This means that people will always be learning new job skills, and schools must become lifelong-learning centers, open 24/7, to people of all ages and all walks of life.

In addition to the many online learning centers and even online universities, there have been many recent advances in research about learning. These include neuroscience, multiple intelligences, brain gym, brain exercises, the science of communication, experiential learning, project based learning, accelerated learning, and even research into how nutrition affects learning.

We prepare for our careers (scientists, engineers, doctors) at school, but do we also learn how to be caring, responsible citizens? Do we learn about the meaning of life and the beauty of art, music, and literature? We need to remember that going to school isn't just about getting a high-paying job. As the philosopher John Dewey points out: "Education is not a preparation for life; education is life itself." As the proverb tells us, "Man cannot live by bread alone". We need to satisfy our deeper needs in life and education gives us an opportunity to do this.

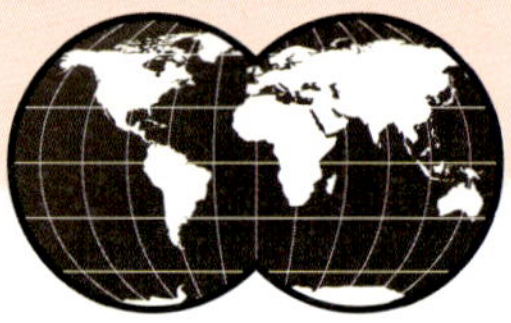

Vocabulary in context

Choose three unfamiliar words from this passage and write them below. Look in the Glossary (▸pages 151–168) for their meanings. Write a new sentence for each word.

word	sentence
1	
2	
3	

There are more reading passages at http://www.finchpark.com/KNUFLE/book-1/unit04/read.html.

Discussion topics

Think about the reading text (▸page 40) and discuss these questions together.
Use the discussion words and phrases in the Word Bank (▸pages 144 – 150).

1. What does '24/7' mean?
2. What is the purpose of education? Explain your opinion.
3. What does 'Man cannot live by bread alone' mean?
4. Would you like to study in an online university? [Yes] Why? [No] Why not?
5. What do you think of the Learning Revolution?

Look at this diagram.
Talk about it with a classmate.

Are you a left-brain thinker?
Are you a right-brain thinker?
Is it possible to mix the two?

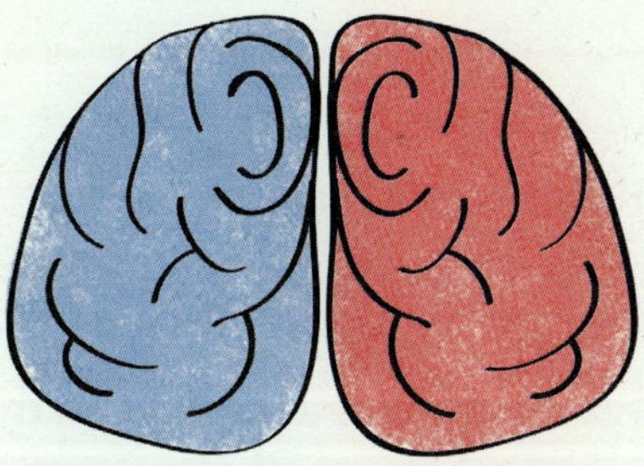

Now look at the words below and SAY the COLORS, not the words.
Your right brain will try to say the color; your left brain will read the word!
Can you do it in less than a minute?

If this test is easy for you, then your right-brain is dominant.
If you cannot do this test in one minute, then your left-brain is dominant.

GREEN YELLOW BLUE
RED BROWN ORANGE
BLACK BLUE PURPLE
BLUE WHITE YELLOW
GREEN ORANGE RED
PURPLE BLUE BLACK

Interacting Our learning styles

Look at your answers on 'My Page' (▶page 37) and write your scores in the table below. What type of learner are you?

Page 37 Question numbers

- Yes, this is true of me. = 5 points
- This is sometimes true of me. = 3 points
- No, this is not really true of me. = 1 point

Write your totals.

Visual	2		3		7		10		15		17		VPS Total =
Auditory	1		5		8		11		13		18		APS Total =
Tactile	4		6		9		12		14		16		TPS Total =

Hints for the Visual Preference Style (VPS) Learner:

- Take notes and make pictures, graphs, or charts.
- Read and study in a well-lit, quiet place.
- Use highlighters for important information.
- Keep a note pad with you at all times.

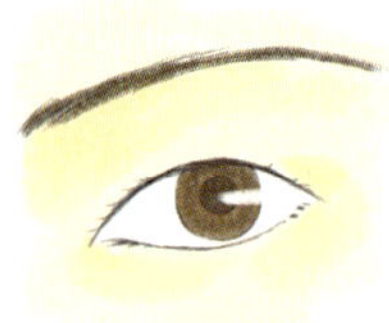

Hints for the Auditory Preference Style (APS) Learner:

- Read your work out loud.
- Brainstorm ideas with other people.
- Make study groups with other students.
- Record class lectures.

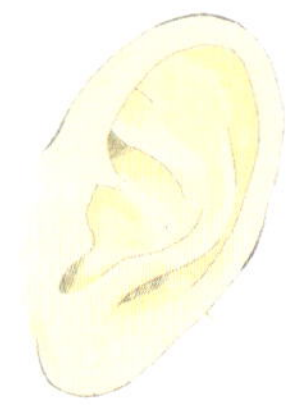

Hints for the Tactile Preference Style (TPS) learner:

- Listen to soft music while studying.
- Study in short periods, for example 30 minutes.
- Use models and real objects to help you learn.
- Clear your desk of unnecessary objects.

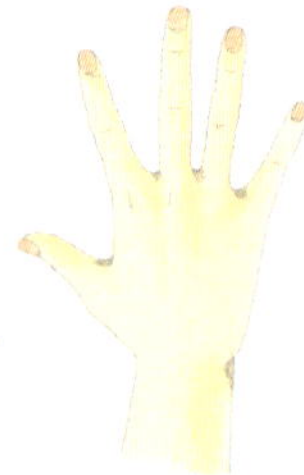

This activity is based on page 31 of *English Reflections*. A.Finch (2010). KNU Press.

Talk to people in the class and find this information:

How many VPS Learners are there in the class? ____________________

How many APS Learners are there in the class? ____________________

How many TPS Learners are there in the class? ____________________

Learning workshop *My study skills*

People who have good study skills learn more effectively. This activity helps you to find out about your study skills and improve them.

Step 1: Exchange your book with a classmate.

Step 2: Ask your classmate the questions below. Check ☑ his/her answers.

	Yes	No
1. Does it take you a long time to learn anything?		
2. If you study as much as you should, do you have time for a social life?		
3. Do you like to study with the radio and TV turned on?		
4. Can you study for a long time without becoming tired?		
5. Do you play with your pencil, daydream, or fall asleep in class?		
6. When you make notes in class, are they difficult to read afterwards?		
7. Do you review your notes regularly during the semester?		
8. When you read a chapter in a textbook, can you remember the content?		
9. Do you know how to find important information in the text?		
10. Do you wish that you could read faster?		
11. Do you find it difficult to get started on writing assignments?		
12. Do you have difficulty in organizing your ideas in a writing assignment?		
13. Do you write your writing assignments the night before they are due?		
14. Do your writing assignments show your best ability?		
15. Do you spend a long time cramming the night before an exam?		
16. Do you forget things in a test, even after you have studied for it?		
17. Do you study in an organized way for a test?		

Step 3: Look at your classmate's answers. Here are some problems that you might find:

- Question 1. Yes, 2. No, 15. Yes, = Time management problems.
- Question 3. Yes, 4. No, 5. Yes, = Concentration problems.
- Question 6. Yes, 7. No, = Listening and note taking problems.
- Question 8. No, 9. No, 10. Yes, = Reading problems.
- Question 11. Yes, 12. Yes, 13. Yes, 14. No, = Writing problems.
- Question 15. Yes, 16. Yes, 17. No, = Exam problems.

Step 4: Talk about your study skills together. How can you improve your study skills? You can find some useful tips here: http://www.finchpark.com/KNUFLE/book-1/unit04/.

Writing workshop *Apostrophes and personal pronouns*

Look at this chart and fill in the empty boxes. The first row has been done for you.

Subject	Object	Apostrophe	Adjective	Possessive
I	me	I'm happy	my	mine
you				
he				
she				
we				
they				

Can you fix the apostrophes and personal pronouns in these sentences? Talk about them together and rewrite them correctly.

1. Thats not mine dog. Im certain about that.

2. Its too late to visit hers now. Shes probably asleep.

3. Were going to Franks party in ours cars.

4. Todays trip is ours first holiday this year. Its a beautiful day.

5. The womens soccer player's had hers first game today.

6. The childrens toy's are in they boxes.

7. This isnt they's house. Its my. Thats there's over there.

The answers are in the **Answer Section** (▸page 170). Find out more about apostrophes and personal pronouns on the website: www.finchpark.com/KNUFLE/book-1/unit04/writing.html.

Writing skills *Order of importance paragraphs*

'Order of importance' paragraphs are similar to listing paragraphs (▸Unit 2). Here is a sample paragraph:

Track 17

How to Study

There are a number of ways to make the study process more effective. The most important thing is to have an open, well-organized study surface, such as a large desk. This helps concentration. The next thing is to have a quiet place to study in. Music and snacks can break the flow of study. The third most important thing is to take a short break every hour. This helps blood circulation and refreshes your mind. If you follow these tips, they will help you make the most of your study time.

The reading passage on page 38 is another 'order of importance' paragraph. Choose one of these two sample paragraphs and fill in the information below:

Main idea ______________________________

First reason ______________________________

____

Second reason ______________________________

____

Third reason ______________________________

____

Conclusion ______________________________

What are the three most important characteristics of the following people?

A good friend	A good teacher	A good student
1	1	1
2	2	2
3	3	3

Check out the order of importance paragraph links on the Unit 4 website ("Writing").

Writing practice *Outlining and first draft*

Choose a topic for your order of importance paragraph:

(your choice)

1. A good job 2. A good student 3. A happy life 4. ____________

Write the topic below (Main idea) and then make an outline for your paragraph (▸ see page 45).

Main idea ____________

First reason ____________

Second reason ____________

Third reason ____________

Conclusion ____________

Now write an order of importance paragraph about your topic.

Draft 1

____

Peer-editing

Exchange books with a classmate and edit his/her first draft. Use the checklist on page 47. Return the book and talk about your first drafts together.

Writing assignment Rewriting and reviewing

Rewrite your paragraph, based on your classmate's editing and your own ideas.

Name: ____________________ Draft 2

Here is a checklist of things to look for when you are peer–editing. You should also use it for self–editing your second draft.

✓	Peer/Self-Editing Checklist	
☐	Capital letters	(**C** – pages 19 and 141)
☐	Punctuation	(**P** – pages 31 and 141)
☐	Apostrophes, pronouns	(**Gr1** - pages 44 and 141)
☐	Paragraph format	(**Para** - pages 7 and 141)

Review corner *Self-assessment: Learning skills*

Write words here that describe your learning skills. Look at the Self-assessment words on page 140 and the Adjectives on page 138.

My learning skills	
Goal-setting	
Planning	
Organizing	
Study skills	
Reflecting	

Review what you have done in this Unit and prepare for the next Unit.

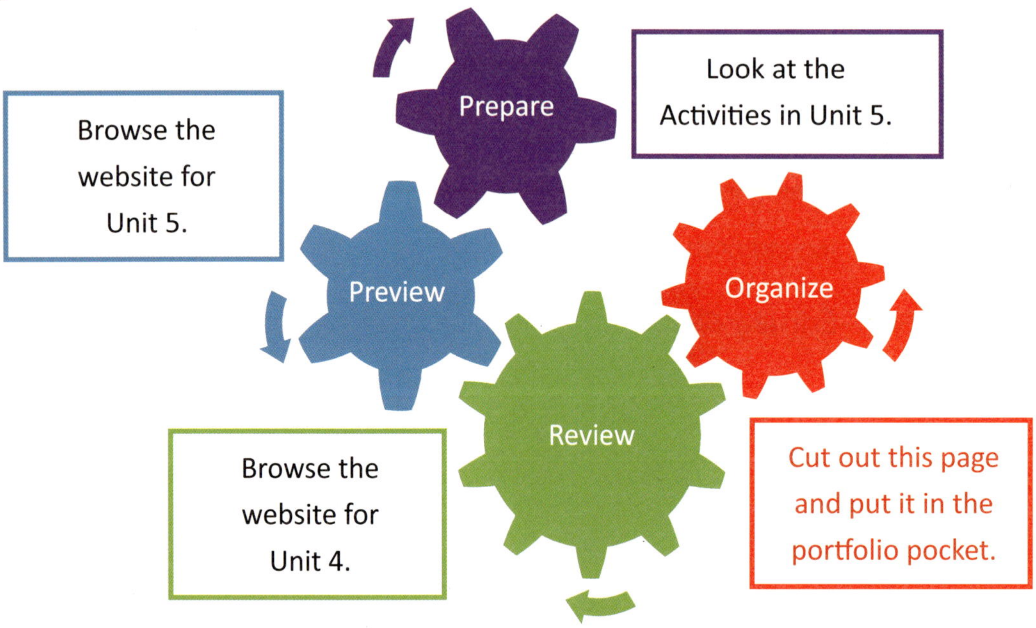

http://www.finchpark.com/KNUFLE/book-1/index.html.

UNIT 5 Festival time

My page *My festivals*

Here are some festivals from around the world. Look at the map and write the numbers of the festivals in front of their names. Two have been done for you.

12	Mardi Gras	2	Edinburgh Festival		Boryeong Mud Festival
	Rio Carnival		Cape Town Festival		Melbourne Arts Festival
	Oktoberfest		Ice Lantern Festival		Valencia Tomato Festival
	HiSeoul Festival		Notting Hill Carnival		Montreal Jazz Festival
	Festival d'Avignon		Sapporo Snow Festival		Marrakesh Popular Arts Festival

The answers are in the **Answer section** at the back of the book.

Talk to a classmate. Do you know about any of these festivals? Talk about festivals in your own country.

> ***Today's quotation***: "You are invited to the festival of this world and your life is blessed." (Rabindranath Tagore)

Reading and discussing (step 1)

Track 18

Read this passage, find vocabulary, and then talk about the discussion topics

Good Clean Fun

Have you ever heard of the Boryeong Mud Festival? The mud from Boryeong contains many minerals and in 1996 a range of cosmetics was made using this mud. Then in 1998 the first Mud Festival was held to tell people about the cosmetics. Since then the festival has become very popular, with more than 2 million visitors each year to this normally quiet seaside town.

Boryeong is on the west coast of Korea, about 200 km south of Seoul. During the festival, which takes place during two weeks of July, mud is taken from the Boryeong mud flats to Daecheon beach, where it is used for mud pools, mud slides, mud skiing, mud wrestling, mud massages, and mud photo competitions. This festival, which began life as a marketing idea, has even been mentioned in *TIME* magazine, which called it "Good clean fun."

Vocabulary in context

Choose two or three unfamiliar words and write them in the table. Find the meanings (Glossary, ▸pages 151–168). Write a sentence for each word.

word	sentence
1	
2	
3	

Discussion topics

1. Would you like to visit this festival? [Yes] Why? [No] Why not?

2. Do you know any modern festivals? Talk about them.

3. If you could start a new festival, what sort of festival would you make?

There are more reading passages at http://www.finchpark.com/KNUFLE/book-1/unit05/read.html.

Reading and discussing (step 2)

Track 19

Read this passage, find vocabulary, and then talk about the discussion topics.

Venice Carnival

The Carnival of Venice is a festival that celebrates the ending of winter and the coming of spring with concerts, grand balls, film shows, and other events. Class differences are forgotten and normal people dress up like the rich and powerful. Everyone hides their true identity by wearing extravagant masks and there is even a contest for the best mask.

The Carnival begins 40 days before the Christian festival of Easter and ends on Shrove Tuesday, the day before Ash Wednesday. These 40 days of Lent are traditionally times of fasting and meditating, when people do not eat meat. The word 'carnevale' probably comes from the Latin 'carne' (meat) and 'vale' (farewell).

The *Carnevale di Venezia* has a long history. It was first mentioned in documents written in 1092, before the Senate of Venice made it an official festival, in 1296. However, it fell out of fashion in the 19th and 20th centuries, until the Italian government decided to revive Italian history and culture and restarted the traditional Carnival. Since then it has become very popular, attracting 30,000 visitors a day, and having a new theme each year.

Vocabulary in context

Choose three unfamiliar words from the passage and write them below. Check the Glossary (▸pages 151–168) for their meanings. Write a sentence for each word.

word	sentence
1	
2	
3	

Discussion topics

1. Can you think of any other Christian festivals? Talk about them.
2. Are there any very old festivals in Korea? Describe them.
3. Have you ever been to a festival? Talk about it.

There are more reading passages at http://www.finchpark.com/KNUFLE/book-1/unit05/read.html.

Reading and discussing (step 3)

Track 20

Read this passage, find vocabulary, and talk about the topics on the next page.

Festival of Life

Every country has its own festivals, celebrating some unique aspect of its culture. In Ireland, for example, people paint their faces, draw shamrocks, wear green clothes, and drink green beer on Saint Patrick's Day. In Brazil, on the other hand, 'Carnaval' is the most famous holiday. This is a time of friendship, freedom, and almost a whole week without work. The many different festivals in the world all bring people together, either for religious reasons, social reasons, or simply for entertainment.

Ancient festivals used to celebrate the gods, the sun, the moon, and the seasons. Spring festivals marked the ending of winter and the renewal of life. Harvest festivals helped people to give thanks for abundant crops. New Year festivals gave families a chance to come together and look forward to spring. These were all times when elderly members of society would tell stories and pass on important traditions. Modern festivals often remind us of these traditions.

Every religion has its festivals, from Buddha's birthday to Easter, Diwali, Ramadan, and Hanukkah. These special times offer an opportunity for believers to renew their faith, as well as celebrating important religious events.

These days, there are lots of modern festivals, including film festivals, flower festivals, cheese festivals, beer festivals, wine festivals, and food festivals. Some strange events have also appeared, such as 'La Tomatina', 'Cheese Rolling', and 'Underwater Cycling'. Whether praying, meditating, throwing tomatoes (Spain), joining in the Oktoberfest (Germany), or participating in the Night of the Radishes (Mexico), festivals provide us with a chance to get in touch with our culture, while expressing our happiness and joy at being alive.

Vocabulary in context

Choose three unfamiliar words from this passage and write them below. Look in the Glossary (▸pages 151–168) for their meanings and write a sentence for each word.

word	sentence
1	
2	
3	

There are more reading passages at http://www.finchpark.com/KNUFLE/book-1/unit05/read.html.

Discussion topics

Think about the reading text (▸page 52) and discuss these questions together. Use the discussion words and phrases in the Word Bank (▸pages 144 – 150).

1. Which festival on page 52 would you like to visit? Why?
2. Are any festivals unique to Korea? Describe them.
3. What is your favorite festival? Talk about it.
4. Are there any festivals in your city? Talk about them.

How many festivals can you think of? Write them below.

Religious festivals	Seasonal festivals	Cultural festivals

What do you think happens in these festivals?

La Tomatina	Santa Lucia Day	HiSeoul Festival
Halloween	Underwater Cycling	The Battle of the Oranges
Oktoberfest	Night of the Radishes	Wife Carrying Championship
Cheese Rolling	Monkey Buffet Festival	Camel Wrestling Championship

Check out the videos on the website for this Unit ("Viewing").

Interacting *Our festival poster*

You are organizing a festival. Make a poster for your festival. Include the festival name, dates, locations, times, special events, contact information, and website. Useful discussion words and phrases are given at the bottom of the page.

Suggesting	Agreeing/disagreeing	Giving an opinion	Direction
Let's ...	I agree.	I think …	here
Why not … ?	I disagree.	I think (that)...	there
I suggest ...	I don't agree.	In my opinion,	opposite
I've an idea.	That's a good idea.	I believe that ...	left
How about … ?	Me too! So do I.	Well, personally,	right
Why don't we … ?	I agree with you there.	It's my opinion that …	above
Have you thought of ...?	That's what I thought.	From my point of view,	below
			between

Look at pages 144-150 for more discussion words and phrases.

Writing workshop Singular/plural, Count/non-count

Discuss the sentences below and write the correct versions underneath.

1. Everyone [has/have] finished their [work/works].

2. None of them [has/have] eaten [much/many] [meat/meats].

3. I spread [some/a few] [butter/butters] on the [slices of bread/breads].

4. There was [few/little] [time/times] to listen to [any/no] [music/musics].

5. We have had [much/lots of] extreme [weather/weathers] recently.

6. There [was/were] [a few/any] [pieces of furniture/furnitures] in the room.

7. It takes [enough/a lot of] [courage/courages] to fight for your [belief/beliefs].

8. [None/No one] of the guests drank [any/no] [wine/wines].

9. Do you drink [enough/as much as] [water/waters] each day?

10. Which [is/are] more important, [leisure/leisures] or [education/educations]?

Quiz corner

Discuss these puzzles and see if you can find the answers.

1. What is in the middle of Paris?
2. How long was the 100 Years War?
3. What happened in 1961 and will not happen again until 6009?

Answers for the Writing Workshop and the Quiz Corner are in the **Answer Section**, at the back of the book.
Check out the 'singular/plural,' 'count/non-count,' and 'subject-verb agreement' links on the website for Unit 5 (Writing).

Writing skills *The comparison paragraph (1)*

Track 21

Here is a sample comparison paragraph. It uses description words (▸page 139) and 'comparison and contrast' words (▸page 147). Write these comparison/contrast words in the correct places in the paragraph:

also	than	unlike	For one thing	on the other hand	For example
also	more	whereas	Then again	For another thing	

Best Friends

Tom and Tim have been friends for a long time, so they have many things in common. ____________, they both like music and movies and they are both morning people. __________, they _____ have their differences. ____________, Tom is left-handed and easy-going, ______ Tim, who is right-handed and quick-tempered. __________, Tom has brown eyes and short, fair hair, __________ Tim is blue-eyed and curly-haired. Tim is _____ taller _____ Tom, and _____ athletic. He likes all sports. Tom, ______________, is rather flat-footed and prefers to read a book or ride his bike.

The answers are in the **Answer Section** at the back of the book.

Talk about these two faces with a classmate.

Similarities	Differences

Check out the comparison paragraph links on the Unit 5 website ("Writing").

Writing skills *The comparison paragraph (2)*

Track 22

The paragraph on page 56 compares two people at the same time. We can also compare topics one after the other. Read the following paragraph and underline the two main topics. Highlight the comparison/contrast words.

Two Film Festivals

The Sundance Film Festival is the largest independent cinema festival in the U.S.A. It is held each year in Park City, Salt Lake City, Ogden, and the Sundance Resort. It began in 1978 with the aim of featuring American-made films. In the 2012 festival, 117 full-length feature films from 30 countries were shown. In comparison, the Busan International Film Festival (BIFF) focuses on new films and directors from Asian Countries. When it began in 1996, it was the first international film festival in Korea. In contrast to the Sundance, the BIFF has only one venue, the Busan Cinema Center. In the 2012 festival, 304 films from 75 countries were shown.

Look at these two rooms with a classmate. Compare them using the location words on page 139 and the words under the pictures.

bigger than	lighter than	as good as	more empty
smaller than	darker than	as large as	more expensive
better than	simpler than	as comfortable as	more attractive
wider than	higher than	as stylish as	more relaxing
narrower than	lower than	as fashionable as	more modern

There are more comparison and contrast words in the **Word Bank**, on page 147.

Writing practice *Brainstorming, outlining and first draft*

Choose a title for your comparison paragraph:

1. High school/university
2. Early bird/night owl
3. Two rooms
4. Two seasons
5. Two cars
6. Two friends
7. ______ (Your own topic)

Brainstorm the characteristics of the two things that you are comparing.

Next, outline the similarities and differences.

Similarities	Differences

Now write a comparison paragraph about your topic.

Draft 1

Peer-editing

Edit your classmate's first draft using the Checklist on page 59. Return the book and talk about your first drafts together.

Writing assignment Rewriting

Rewrite your paragraph, based on your classmate's editing and your own ideas.

Name: ______________________ Draft 2

Here is a checklist of things to look for when you are peer-editing. You should also use it for self-editing your second draft.

✓	Peer/Self-Editing Checklist	
☐	Capital letters	(**C** – pages 19 and 141)
☐	Punctuation	(**P** – pages 31 and 141)
☐	Apostrophes, pronouns	(**Gr1** - pages 44 and 141)
☐	Singular/plural, count/non-count	(**Gr2** - pages 55 and 141)
☐	Paragraph format	(**Para** - pages 7 and 141)

Review corner *Self-assessment: Social skills*

Do you get along well with other people? Self-assess your social skills below.

My social skills	Team work	Consideration	Leadership	Body language	Positive attitude
	4	4	4	4	4
	3	3	3	3	3
	2	2	2	2	2
	1	1	1	1	1

My total ___ /20			
	I need to be more of a team player.	yes	no
	I need to be more considerate of other people.	yes	no
	I need to think about my leadership skills.	yes	no
	I need to think about my body language.	yes	no
	I need to be more positive with other people.	yes	no

Review what you have done in this Unit and prepare for the next Unit.

http://www.finchpark.com/KNUFLE/book-1/index.html

UNIT 6 The stuff of legend

My page My myths

Here are some characters from Greek myths.
Can you match the characters with the items?

Character	Item
1. Achilles'	adventure
2. Ariadne's	arrow
3. Cupid's	box
4. Hercules'	complex
5. Icarus'	fire
6. Medusa's	hand
7. Midas'	head
8. Minotaur's	heel
9. Odysseus'	maze
10. Oedipus	stone
11. Pandora's	tasks
12. Prometheus'	thread
13. Sisyphus'	wings

The answers are in the **Answer Section** at the back of the book.

These characters and their items have special meanings for us. Talk about these meanings together. What does the Minotaur's maze mean to you?

***Today's quotation*:** "Give me a place to stand and I will move the earth." (Archimedes)

Reading and discussing (step 1)

Track 23

Read this passage, find vocabulary, and then talk about the discussion topics.

Korean Dramas

Do you like watching dramas? Since the Korean Wave (also known as *Hallyu*) began with the film *Shiri* in 1999, Korean drama fever has spread all round the world. The first of these new dramas was *Winter Sonata*, which was aired in Korea in 2002, in Japan in 2003, and as an anime series in 2009. The main male actor, Bae Yong-joon, is known as 'Yonsama' in Japan and thousands of Japanese visitors visit Korea to see the film locations each year.

Winter Sonata is an example of the first main genre of Korean dramas – the soap opera. In this genre, there are often complex love triangles. On the other hand, *Dae Jang Geum* and *Jumong* are examples of the second main genre – historical dramas. Both types of Korean dramas have interesting plots and well-developed characters.

Vocabulary in context

Choose two or three unfamiliar words and write them in the table. Find the meanings (Glossary, ▸pages 151–168). Write a sentence for each word.

word	sentence
1	
2	
3	

Discussion topics

1. Talk about any Korean Wave dramas that you have seen.

2. Do you like Korean dramas? [Yes] Why? [No] Why not?

3. What do you think of *Hallyu*, including K-pop?

There are more reading passages at http://www.finchpark.com/KNUFLE/book-1/unit06/read.html.

Reading and discussing (step 2)

Track 24

Read this passage, find vocabulary, and then talk about the discussion topics.

Dreamtime

There are many Australian myths, also known as Dreamtime stories. One of these aborigine tales explains why the koala bear has no tail. Once upon a time there was a terrible drought. All the animals were dying of thirst, except Koala, who never seemed to get thirsty. Therefore, the animals and birds decided to watch him day and night, to find out why he was not thirsty. After some time, Lyre-bird saw Koala hanging upside-down from a branch by his long tail. He was drinking water from a tiny pool between two branches.

Lyre-bird realized that the tree might be hollow and full of water. However, he couldn't reach the branch where Koala was hanging. He didn't have an axe to cut down the tree, so he found a firestick and set the tree alight. In the end, the burning bark broke into pieces and water burst out like a fountain. All the animals jumped into the water and drank their fill. Koala had to jump into another tree to escape from the fire, but his tail burned up and never grew back.

Vocabulary in context

Choose three unfamiliar words from the passage and write them below. Check the Glossary (▸pages 151–168) for their meanings. Write a new sentence for each word.

word	sentence
1	
2	
3	

Discussion topics

1. Can you think of a Korean animal myth? Tell the story.
2. Do you know any modern myths (anime, cartoons, etc.)? Tell us about them.
3. Do you know any myths and legends from other countries?

There are more reading passages at http://www.finchpark.com/KNUFLE/book-1/unit06/read.html.

Reading and discussing (step 3)

Track 25

Read this passage, find vocabulary, and talk about the topics on the next page.

The Legend of King Arthur

The story of King Arthur is an old English legend. It tells us that Arthur was the first son of King Pendragon and heir to the English throne. However, these were dangerous times and the king's magician, Merlin, told the king that Arthur should be taken from the castle and raised in a secret place.

When the king died, noblemen fought over who would be the next king. Merlin used his magic to set a sword in a stone. On the sword were these words: 'Whoever pulls this sword out of the stone will be king of all England'. At first, no one could pull the sword out, until the young Arthur innocently withdrew it for another person to use in a tournament. Soon after this, he became king.

Later, Arthur fought many great battles, and was badly wounded by King Pellinore. Merlin took him to a safe place and Lady Guinevere looked after him. Then they went to a lake, where an arm came out of the water, holding the sword Excalibur. This sword protected him for the rest of his life.

Arthur built a strong castle at a place called Camelot, where his knights met around a Round Table. They carried out many good deeds and searched for a lost treasure, called the Holy Grail.

In the end, civil war broke out and Arthur was mortally wounded. As he lay dying, he asked Sir Bedivere to throw Excalibur back into the lake, where a hand reached out of the water and caught it. Finally, Arthur was put on a boat and floated down river to the isle of Avalon, where three mysterious maidens treated his wounds. According to the legend, his body was never found.

Vocabulary in context

Choose three unfamiliar words from this passage and write them below. Look in the Glossary (▸pages 151–168) for their meanings and write a sentence for each word.

word	sentence
1	
2	
3	

There are more reading passages at http://www.finchpark.com/KNUFLE/book-1/unit06/read.html.

Discussion topics

Think about the reading text (▸page 64) and discuss these questions together. Use the discussion words and phrases in the Word Bank (▸pages 144 – 150).

1. Do you think King Arthur existed? Explain your opinion.
2. Can you think of any Korean historical legends? Talk about them.
3. What do you think of *The Three Kingdoms*? Is it still meaningful?
4. Which legendary person would you like to talk to? Why?
5. If you could be a famous person for one day, who would you be? Why?

Who are these people? What do you know about them? Why can they be called 'legends in their own lifetime'?

The answers are in the **Answer Section** at the back of the book.

Interacting *Our Soap Opera*

Soap operas look at issues that normal people face. What do you think the people are saying in this comic strip? Write your words in the speech bubbles.

Make your own plot, with sequencers, people, actions, and conjunctions.

sequencers	people	actions	conjunctions
First, →	Mario →	loves, marries, leaves →	and
Then,	Julian	doesn't know that	but
Next,	Petra	has an affair with	or
After that,	Celia	becomes bankrupt	so
In the end,	Kyle	becomes terminally ill	because
Finally,	Amanda	is in a coma in hospital	however
	Dr. Sinclair	goes blind, dies, has a car crash	therefore

For example: First, Mario loves Petra, but she leaves him for Kyle.

Check out the "Viewing" links on the Unit 6 website.

Writing workshop *Spelling*

Angela has written in her diary, but she needs to check the spelling. Write "**Sp**" above her errors and write the correct words underneath.

Sp Sp
Angela's Dairy, April twelth
Diary twelfth

The whether was fine this after-noon so I had a walk in the prak. I often go there accept when its rainning and sometime I stay untill evening. Its not to far and the exercize does me good. Toady I met my nieghbor, Janice. She has been unwel, but to-day she looked very helthy. We gossipped for housr as we wondered thrugh the treees and sharred our news.

How about these words? Which ones are correct? Talk about them together.

✗ beleive	✓ believe
exceed	excede
independant	independent
judgment	judgement
licence	license
receive	recieve

calendar	calender
greatful	grateful
accomodation	accommodation
liesure	leisure
pastime	pasttime
✓ schedule	✗ scedule

The answers for this Writing Workshop are in the **Answer Section**, at the back of the book.
There are some helpful links about spelling on the website for Unit 6 ("Writing").

Writing skills *The time order paragraph (1)*

Track 26

Time order paragraphs describe things that have happened and often tell a story. Here is a sample paragraph. How many sequencing words can you find (▸page 150)?

It's Magic.

Earvin 'Magic' Johnson was born in 1959 in Michigan and has become a legend in his lifetime. First, he played for the local high school team when he was 15 years old. After that, he went to Michigan State University, where his team won the NCAA tournament of 1978-79. Next he joined the Los Angeles Lakers in 1979, helping them win 5 NBA championships. Then he retired from basketball in 1991, but returned in 1992, playing for the US 'Dream Team' in the Barcelona Olympics. Finally, he was elected to the Pro Basketball Hall of Fame in 2002. Since then, he has given his time and money to helping young people.

Here are some events in the life of Vincent van Gogh. Choose some events and make a time order paragraph.

1853 Born, Groot-Zundert, Holland
1869 Worked for an art dealer in London.
1879 Missionary in Belgium. Decided to become a painter.
1881 Holland. Proposed to his cousin. She refused.
1882 The Hague, South Holland. Began painting in oil.
1886 Paris. Lived with his brother.
1888 Arles, south of France. Some time in a mental hospital.
1890 Sold his first painting. Shot himself.

Writing skills The time order paragraph (2)

Track 27

Time order paragraphs can describe daily routines, like a diary. Highlight the sequencing words in this sample paragraph:

> A Day in the Life of a Designer
>
> Time-management is very important for me, since my typical day is very busy. First of all, I wake at 5:30 am, get up, and make a pot of coffee. Then, after I have showered, I have breakfast at about 6 o'clock and check my e-mails and my blog. Next, at 7 o'clock I check my to-do list for the day and go to the gym. Then, when I get to the office at 9:30, I am ready to do some good work. I often have a working lunch at 1 pm and check my accounts in the afternoon. Later, when I've finished work for the day, I have a drink with friends or work on new ideas at home. Finally, I get to sleep around 10 pm. Another day is over.

What happens in your typical day? Write the events in order, along with sequencing words (▶page 150).

Time	Sequence words	Events

Check out the Unit 6 website ("Writing") for links about time order paragraphs.

Writing practice Brainstorming, outlining and first draft

Choose a topic for your time order paragraph:

1. My Soap Opera (▸page 66) 2. A Biography (▸page 68)
3. My Day (▸page 69) 4. ____________ (Your choice)

Now brainstorm your ideas and organize the events.

Ideas	Sequence words	Events

Next, write a time order paragraph about your topic.

Draft 1

Peer-editing

Exchange books with a classmate. Edit his/her first draft using the Marking Code on page 141. Return the book and talk about your first drafts together.

Writing assignment Rewriting and teacher-editing

Rewrite your paragraph, based on your classmate's editing and your own ideas.
Cut out this page and give this second draft to the teacher for editing.

Name: ____________________ Second draft

Teacher's Feedback

When you get your second draft back, write your final draft on the next page.

Writing assignment *Final draft*

Rewrite your paragraph, based on the teacher's feedback (▸page 71).

Final draft

Review what you have done in this Unit and prepare for the next Unit.

Review	• Browse the website for Unit 6.
Preview	• Browse the website for Unit 7.
Prepare	• Look at the activities in Unit 7.
Organize	• Put this page in the portfolio pocket.

http://www.finchpark.com/KNUFLE/book-1/

UNIT 7 In a nutshell

My page What do I eat?

Think about the food you eat each day and fill in the table below.

My Daily Food Intake	breakfast	lunch	dinner	snacks
Fats, oils, sweets				
dairy products (milk, yogurt, cheese)				
fish, seafood, meat, beans, nuts, seeds				
fruit and vegetables				
cereals, bread, rice, pasta, noodles				
water and others (tea, coffee, soft drinks)				

Talk with a classmate about your daily food intake.

Do you eat enough vegetables?
Do you eat many snacks and sweet foods?
Do you eat regularly?
Do you ever skip a meal? Why?
Do you drink enough water?

Today's quotation: "An apple a day keeps the doctor away." (Proverb)

Reading and discussing (step 1)

Track 28

Read this passage, find vocabulary, and then talk about the discussion topics.

Brain Food

Believe it or not, the food we eat affects not only our body but also our emotions and our mind. Eating the right food can help you concentrate, keep you motivated, enlarge your memory, reduce stress and even stop your brain from aging. An 8-month 'Food for the Brain Project' at an elementary school in the UK resulted in better grades, attitudes, behavior, attention, and learning abilities in the students.

Here is a list of top brain foods:

1. Broccoli, spinach, kale
2. Salmon, tuna
3. Whole grains
4. Seeds (flax, sunflower, sesame)
5. Bananas
6. Real yogurt
7. Walnuts, mixed nuts
8. Beans
9. Blueberries, strawberries
10. Vegetable salad
11. Real coffee
12. Real chocolate

Vocabulary in context

Choose two or three unfamiliar words and write them in the table. Find the meanings (Glossary, ▸pages 151–168). Write a sentence for each word.

word	sentence
1	
2	
3	

Discussion topics

1. Do you eat brain food? [Yes] Why? [No] Why not?
2. Have you heard of 'color foods' and 'comfort foods'? Talk about them.
3. How are 'fast food,' 'junk food,' and 'healthy food' different?

There are more reading passages at http://www.finchpark.com/KNUFLE/book-1/unit07/read.html.

Reading and discussing (step 2)

Track 29

Read this passage, find vocabulary, and then talk about the discussion topics.

How to Make Fried Rice

Fried rice is a healthy dish that is easy to make. You can also add more ingredients if you want to. Here is a recipe for 4 to 6 people:

Ingredients:

- 1-2 green onions
- 1 teaspoon of salt
- ½ cup of peas
- 4 tablespoons of vegetable oil
- 4 cups of cooked rice
- 2 eggs
- 1 carrot
- Pepper to taste
- 1-2 tablespoons of soy sauce

First of all, cook the rice until it is tender. Then drain it and leave it to cool. Next, you need to wash and chop the green onion(s) and peel and chop the carrot. After that, lightly beat the eggs in a small bowl, with the salt and pepper. Next, heat 2 tablespoons of oil in a frying pan. Add the eggs and stir them until they are cooked. Then put them in a dish to cool. Later, cut them into strips. Meanwhile, stir-fry the carrot for I minute, with 2 tablespoons of oil. Add the green onions, the peas, and the rice. Cook and stir for 3-4 minutes, using chopsticks or a wooden spoon. Finally, add the egg strips and the soy sauce. When the mixture is hot, serve it immediately.

Vocabulary in context

Choose some unfamiliar words from the passage and write them below. Check the Glossary (▸pages 151–168) for their meanings. Write a sentence for each word.

word	sentence
1	
2	
3	

Discussion topics

1. Do you ever cook your meals? What do you like to cook?
2. How often do you eat home-cooked food? How about fast food?
3. Do you eat a balanced diet? [Yes] What do you eat? [No] Why not?

There are more reading passages at http://www.finchpark.com/KNUFLE/book-1/unit07/read.html.

Reading and discussing (step 3)

Track 30

Read this passage and fill in the missing words. Next find vocabulary. Finally, talk about the topics on the next page.

You Are What You Eat

Every part of our body needs healthy food in order to maintain itself and stay strong. The brain, lungs, heart, liver, stomach, skin, and bones need grains, vegetables, fruits, oils, dairy foods, beans and nuts every day. These give us carbohydrates (for energy), vitamins, fiber (for digestion), nutrients, fats, calcium, and protein. If we want to keep our bodies healthy and functioning well, we need to be careful about what we eat!

I have four valves, which pump blood around your body. First, it goes to the lungs, where it takes in oxygen and then it goes around the body and returns to me. I need protein in order to grow and be strong. I am called the h............... Without me, your body cannot function.

We have a hard outer layer and a spongy inner layer and we are made of protein, minerals and vitamins. We protect the inner organs, support your body against gravity, produce blood cells, allow you to move, and store important minerals. We need calcium and vitamin D. We are called b................. . Without us, your body cannot function.

You control us when you lift things, but most of us carry on without you thinking about us at all. We are all made of thousands of small fibers, which together make an elastic tissue. We need protein, vegetables, fruit, carbohydrates, and healthy fats. We are called m................. . Without us, your body cannot function.

Vocabulary in context

Choose three unfamiliar words from this passage and write them below. Look in the Glossary (▸pages 151–168) for their meanings and write a sentence for each word.

word	sentence
1	
2	
3	

There are more reading passages at http://www.finchpark.com/KNUFLE/book-1/unit07/read.html.

Discussion topics

Think about the reading text (▸page 76) and discuss these questions together.

1. Do you agree that 'You are what you eat'? Explain your opinion.
2. Do you prefer 'slow food' or fast food? Explain your reasons.
3. What is obesity? What is anorexia nervosa? Are they a problem in Korea?
4. How can food help us to achieve a healthy body and a healthy mind?

Do you eat a healthy diet? Answer this questionnaire to find out.

1. How many cups of water do you drink a day?	3 or less	4 to 7	8 or more
2. How many cups of coffee do you drink a day?	6 or more	3 to 5	2 or less
3. How often do you eat fried food?	usually	often	rarely
4. How many servings of fruit & vegetables (plus natural juice) do you have each day?	2 or less	3 to 4	5 or more
5. How often do you eat fast food?	usually	sometimes	rarely
6. How often do you eat fish?	rarely	sometimes	often
7. How many eggs do you eat each week?	4 or more	2 or 3	1 or none
8. How many servings of milk, cheese, or red meat do you have each day?	8 or more	3 to 7	2 or less
9. How many sugary foods and drinks (plus sugar in coffee) do you have each day?	8 or more	3 to 7	2 or less

Too much fat and sugar and too many processed foods can lead to illness and health problems. Think about changing your eating habits.

You probably think about what you eat. However, you need to think about what you should change in order to stay healthy.

You already know that what you eat affects your health. If you have answers in the other columns, however, think about how to improve your diet.

Interacting A healthy diet

You have been asked to choose the lunch menu for the school cafeteria next week. Make the meals healthy (▸pages 74, 76) and delicious. Include all the food types (▸page 73).

Lunch menu

	Main dishes	Side dishes	Desserts
Monday			
Tuesday			
Wednesday			
Thursday			
Friday			

There are lots of discussion phrases in the Word Bank (▸pages 144 – 150).

Quiz corner

Discuss these riddles and see if you can find the answers.

1. What is the answer to this multiplication problem?
   111,111,111 X 111,111,111 =
2. What are two things you cannot eat for dinner?

The answers are in the **Answer Section** at the back of the book.
There are more quizzes on the website for this Unit ("Games & Puzzles").

Writing workshop *Prepositions*

Track 31

A concordancer shows authentic language. It can be very helpful for finding collocations. Read the 'concordancer' paragraph below and fill in the missing prepositions. Here is the box described in the passage:

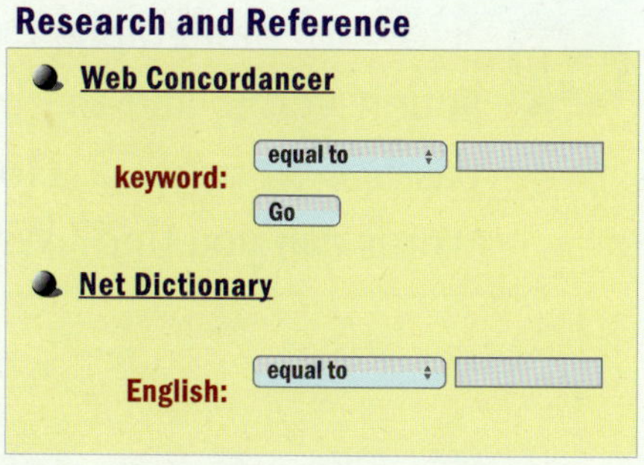

Here are the prepositions used in the passage. Some of them are used more than once.

Above	center of	to the left	as	by	in	on	with
Below	middle of	to the right	at	for	of	to	Underneath

How to use a concordancer

First of all, you need to go ______ the Virtual Language Centre site online. You can find this ______ http://vlc.polyu.edu.hk. This is a free site. You don't have to log ______. When the page loads, you will see a box ______ the ______ the screen. ______ the box are the words "Research and Reference." ______ these words, ______ the top ______ the box, are the words "Web Concordancer." ______ are three white boxes ______, and the word "keyword" ______. If you click ______ the arrow ______ the "equal to" box, the words "starts with," "ends with," and "contains," appear. When you are looking ______ a word or phrase, you can choose one ______ these options. Then you enter your search word or phrase ______ the box ______ the right, and click ______ "Go." Then you will see a screen ______ your search item ______ the ______ the page, ______ blue, surrounded ______ black text. This is a good way ______ finding collocations and seeing a word or phrase ______ it is used ______ real life.

The answers for this Writing Workshop are in the **Answer Section**, at the back of the book. For information about concordancers and prepositions check out the website for Unit 7 ("Writing").

Writing skills *The 'How to' paragraph (1)*

'How to' paragraphs explain how to do something. They use sequencing words, action verbs, and the basic verb form (add, stir, mix, etc). Look at the 'how to' passage on page 75. How many action verbs can you find? How many sequencing words can you find? Write them in the box below:

Here are the ingredients for a tomato sandwich. Make a 'how to' paragraph together, using action verbs and sequencing words (▸page 150). Remember to have a topic sentence and a conclusion sentence. You can have different ingredients if you wish.

Here are the action verbs and sequencing words from page 75. Did you find them all?

add	chop	cut	heat	peel	serve	stir-fry
beat	cook	drain	leave	put	stir	wash

later	then	finally	first of all
next	when	after that	meanwhile

Writing skills The 'How to' paragraph (2)

Track 32

Here is another 'how to' paragraph. This one is about staying healthy.
Underline the action verbs and highlight the sequencing words (▸page 150).

How to Stay Healthy in College

When they start college, many students don't think about their health and get sick easily. Here are a few steps that help us to stay healthy. First, eat 3 meals a day. Second, sleep 7 to 8 hours every night. Third, exercise at least 30 minutes a day. Then make sure you eat a balanced diet, including multivitamins. This will give you a healthy heart, brain, and immune system. Next, keep clean! Wash your hands often and brush your teeth 2 or 3 times a day. Finally, drink 6 to 12 glasses of water each day. These simple steps can help you enjoy your college life.

Here are some pictures that explain how to wash our hands. Write the sequencing words and the action verbs for the pictures. There are some action verbs at the bottom of the page that you can use.

Sequencing words	Action verbs
1	
2	
3	
4	
5	
6	

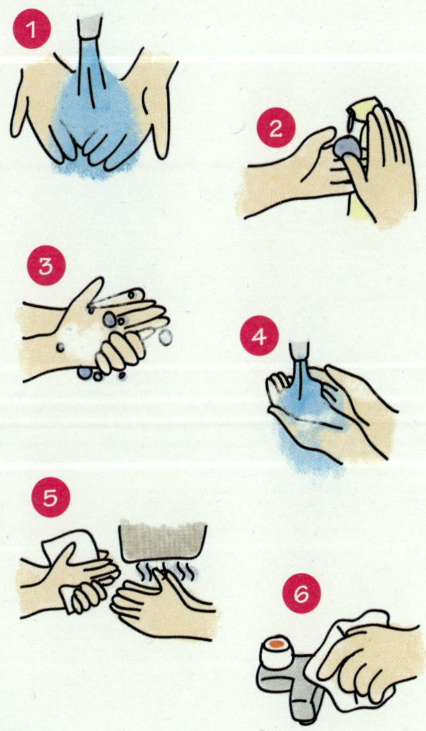

clean	get	rinse	turn on	wash
dry	put	rub	turn off	wipe

There are more 'How to' paragraph activities on the website for Unit 7 ("Writing").

Writing practice

Brainstorming, outlining and first draft

Choose a topic for your paragraph.

1. How to drive a car
2. How to cook ....
3. How to make friends
4. ________________ (Your choice)

Brainstorm your ideas, then choose the sequencing words and the action verbs.

Ideas

Sequencing words	Action verbs

Now write your 'how to' paragraph.

Draft 1

____

____

____

____

____

____

____

____

Peer-editing

Exchange books with a classmate. Edit his/her first draft using the Checklist on page 83 or the Marking Code on page 141. Return the book and talk about your first drafts together.

Writing practice *Rewriting*

Rewrite your paragraph, based on your classmate's editing and your own ideas.

Name: ____________________ Draft 2

Here is a checklist of things to look for when you are peer-editing. You should also use it for self-editing your second draft.

✓	Peer/Self-Editing Checklist	
☐	Capital letters	(**C** – pages 19 and 141)
☐	Punctuation	(**P** – pages 31 and 141)
☐	Apostrophes, personal pronouns	(**Gr1** - pages 44 and 141)
☐	Singular/plural, count/non-count	(**Gr2** - pages 55 and 141)
☐	Prepositions	(**Pr** – pages 79 and 141)
☐	Paragraph format	(**Para** - pages 7 and 141)

Review corner *Self-assessment: Confidence*

How confident are you? Rate yourself in the following chart.

1 = not confident at all; **2** = so-so; **3** = confident

	How confident are you when ...	1	2	3
1.	... speaking English in class with other students?	○	○	○
2.	... speaking English with the teacher?	○	○	○
3.	... speaking English in a test?	○	○	○
4.	... speaking English outside of class (foreigners, travel abroad)?	○	○	○
5.	... writing English in class (first draft)?	○	○	○
6.	... writing English out of class (final draft)?	○	○	○
7.	... writing English in a test (paragraph, essay)?	○	○	○
8.	... listening to English in class (teacher, students)?	○	○	○
9.	... listening to English outside of class (TV, Internet, movies)?	○	○	○
10.	... reading English in class (textbook, instructions)?	○	○	○
11.	... reading English outside of class (Internet, newspapers)?	○	○	○
12.	... giving a presentation in English?	○	○	○
	Total			

I need to improve my confidence in:

Review what you have done in this Unit and prepare for the next Unit.

Review	• Browse the website for Unit 7.
Preview	• Browse the website for Unit 8.
Prepare	• Look at the activities in Unit 8
Organize	• Cut out this page and put it in the portfolio pocket.

http://www.finchpark.com/KNUFLE/book-1/

UNIT 8 All for one

My page My culture

Look at the table below and fill in your cultural profile.

	My cultural profile	Different culture profile
religion		
music		
language		
environment		
staple food		
customs		
clothing style		
arts and sports		
cultural symbols		

Now choose one of these cultures and fill in the 'different culture profile.'

African	Australian	Chinese	Indian	Mexican
American	Canadian	European	Japanese	Middle Eastern

Talk with a classmate.

Which culture did you choose?
How is it different from your culture?
How is it similar to your culture?
What do we mean by 'culture'?

Today's quotation: "We have become not a melting pot but a beautiful mosaic. Different people, different beliefs, different yearnings, different hopes, different dreams." (Jimmy Carter, ex-president of the USA)

Reading and discussing (step 1)

Track 33

Read this passage, find vocabulary, and then talk about the discussion topics.

Changing Cultures

Think about your country's culture. Was it the same 10 years ago? How about 50 years ago? How about 100 years ago? Technology has changed our cultures and our ways of life. Many things that we use every day were just ideas not long ago.

On the one hand, cultures come and go. The Persian, Egyptian, Greek, and Mayan cultures were all powerful at one time, before they disappeared. On the other hand, we need to respect the old traditions and customs. Our ancestors knew about farming and herbal medicine. They also respected old people and believed in morals. Do we want to lose their culture? Do we want to live in a global village with the same culture and the same customs? Do we want to speak the same world language? Is change always good?

Vocabulary in context

Choose two or three unfamiliar words and write them in the table. Find the meanings (Glossary, ▸pages 151–168). Write a sentence for each word.

word	sentence
1	
2	
3	

Discussion topics

1. How is your culture different from 10 years ago? 100 years ago?

2. Which traditional customs do you want to keep? Why?

3. Discuss the advantages and disadvantages of living in a global village.

There are more reading passages at http://www.finchpark.com/KNUFLE/book-1/unit08/read.html.

Reading and discussing (step 2)

Track 34

Read this passage, find vocabulary, and then talk about the discussion topics.

Hopi Indians

Up to now, history has been about battles, generals, kings and noblemen. However, historians are now thinking about women, ethnic minorities, poor people, sick people and old people. From their point of view, history is quite different.

If we look at the Hopi Indians, for example, we find that they had a well-developed society long before the white men arrived. Hopi means *The Peaceful People*, and the idea of peace is deep in the culture. The Hopi religion is anti-war and Hopi Indians live in harmony with nature. Unlike most others, their culture centers on the women. Children join the mother's clan when they are born. The Hopi are also skilled in growing corn, cotton, beans, squash, and tobacco in the middle of the desert.

Today, they live on a reservation in North Arizona, where they struggle to continue their way of life and teach it to their children. As the world becomes globalized, minorities like the Hopi are dying out, along with their cultures and languages. As a result, mankind is in danger of losing the knowledge, legends and crafts that have been preserved for thousands of years.

Vocabulary in context

Choose some unfamiliar words from the passage and write them below. Check the Glossary (▶pages 151–168) for their meanings. Write a new sentence for each word.

word	sentence
1	
2	
3	

Discussion topics

1. How is the Hopi culture different to your culture?

2. Do you know about any ethnic minorities? Talk about them.

3. What can we learn from our ancestors?

There are more reading passages at http://www.finchpark.com/KNUFLE/book-1/unit08/read.html.

Reading and discussing (step 3)

Track 35

Read this passage, find vocabulary, and then discuss the topics on the next page.

The Melting Pot

As the saying goes, variety is the spice of life. America is a diverse society, since everyone (apart from the indigenous Indians) is either an immigrant or has ancestors who have emigrated from other countries. Immigration continues even today, as people try to escape persecution, poverty, or the effects of climate change.

The resulting 'melting pot' of people from diverse cultures can be good for everyone if they can live in peace and harmony, respecting and understanding each other as equal human beings. However, there is a danger that ancient customs and languages can be lost when people move away from their ancestral homes. The Global Village threatens to make everyone speak the same language, wear the same clothes and have the same values. Of the 6,900 languages currently spoken around the world, many are dying out, as young people switch to World Languages instead of those of their parents.

Because of this problem, multilingualism and minority languages are being encouraged in schools. Governments are also helping many ethnic groups to preserve their ancient ways of life and teach their traditional crafts and life-skills to modern citizens who have lost them.

Diversity is important for any species to survive, and biodiversity (the existence of many different life forms) is important for the health of the Earth. However, scientists are worried that biodiversity is disappearing, due to the destruction of animal habitats and rapid environmental change. Modern farming methods and genetically modified (GM) foods have also resulted in less genetic biodiversity. Because of this, 2010 was named the International Year of Biodiversity.

Vocabulary in context

Choose three unfamiliar words from this passage and write them below. Look in the Glossary (▸pages 151–168) for their meanings and write a sentence for each word.

word	sentence
1	
2	
3	

There are more reading passages at http://www.finchpark.com/KNUFLE/book-1/unit08/read.html.

Discussion topics

Think about the reading text (▸page 88) and discuss these questions together.

1. Is Korea a diverse society? [Yes] Give examples. [No] Why not?
2. Do you think everyone should learn English? Explain your opinion.
3. Do you know any ancient customs? Describe them.
4. What do you think about GM food and organic food? Explain your ideas.

Here are six traditional values that make up the American Dream. What are the traditional values of your society?

American Traditional Values	Our Traditional Values
1. **Individual freedom:** Freedom of speech, religion, and assembly (holding meetings) and individual privacy.	1.
2. **Self-reliance:** Individuals should take care of themselves and not depend on other people or on the state.	2.
3. **Equality of opportunity:** Hard work should lead to success, regardless of race, gender, or wealth.	3.
4. **Competition:** Success must be earned through competing with and beating other people.	4.
5. **Material wealth:** Possessions are the natural reward for hard work and a mark of social status.	5.
6. **Hard work:** Everyone should work hard to be successful.	6.

Check out the "Listening" links on the website for this Unit.

Interacting *Cultural differences*

Look at the two pictures below. They show differences between the eating habits of eastern and western cultures.

East

West

Can you think of any differences between eastern and western cultures? Draw your pictures in the boxes below and then talk about the differences together.

There are lots of useful discussion phrases in the **Word Bank**, on pages 144 to 150.

Quiz corner

Talk about this puzzle together.

- Six glasses are standing next to each other.
- Glasses 1, 2, and 3 are full of water. Glasses 4, 5, and 6 are empty.
- Can you move the glasses so that there are no full glasses standing next to each other and no empty glasses standing next to each other?
- You can only use one hand. The other hand should be behind your back.
- How many glasses do you need to move? What is the smallest number of actions that your hand needs to make?

The answer is in the **Answer Section** at the back of the book.

Writing workshop Articles

Track 36

Articles tell us whether nouns are definite (the hat) or indefinite (a hat). They are not used when the noun is general or plural (Which hat do you want? We're out of hats.). Fill in the correct articles (the, a, an, X) in the paragraph below.

Going Through ____ Customs and ____ Immigration Control

When you travel by ____ air to ____ foreign country, there is ____ process that you have to follow before you can board ____ plane. On arrival at ____ airport, ____ first thing you need to do is to check-in and get ____ boarding pass. Once you have your boarding pass you can proceed to ____ security check. After you have been through ____ security you come to ____ customs control, where your passport is checked. You are now free to enter ____ departure lounge, while you wait to board your flight. In order to complete ____ whole process in ____ time, it is ____ good idea to arrive at ____ airport at least two hours before your flight takes off.

Many phrases use the … of:

1. I went to the Island of Dokdo and had the time of my life.
2. ___ Queen ___ England understands ___ value ___ education.
3. ___ President ___ France spoke about ___ benefits ___ technology.
4. He is ___ Speaker ___ ___ House ___ Representatives.
5. ___ joy ___ being alive is at ___ top ___ my list of good things.

Chose the correct articles for the following phrases.

1. Beethoven was ______________ composer. (famous/a famous/the famous)
2. This is not ______________ question. (difficult/a difficult/the difficult)
3. She speaks ______________ well. (French/a French/the French)
4. We had ______________ good weather last week. (very/a very/the very)
5. She is in ______________ health for an 80-year old. (good/a good/the good)
6. He comes from ______________. (Texas/the Texas)
7. ______________ Hallasan is the highest in Korea. (Mount/A Mount/The Mount)
8. ___________ is not ___________. (Spider/A spider/The spider)(insect/an insect/the insect)

The answers to the activities on this page are in the **Answer Section** at the back of the book.
There are more 'Articles' activities on the website for Unit 8 ("Writing").

Writing skills *The process paragraph (1)*

Process paragraphs describe how things happen. They use the present tense to describe natural processes (the weather, the water-cycle, etc.) and man-made processes (making coffee, making steel, making wine, etc.).

There is a man-made process paragraph on page 91 (*Going through Customs and Immigration Control*). Here is another one (*Making Paper*). However, the sentences are in the wrong order. Can you match them to the paragraph parts? The pictures at the bottom give you a hint.

Paragraph parts

- Title
- Topic sentence
- Body sentence 1
- Body sentence 2
- Body sentence 3
- Body sentence 4
- Conclusion sentence

Sentences

- First, trees used for papermaking are harvested, the bark is removed and the trees are cut into 1-inch pieces.
- After it has dried, the finished paper is wound onto rolls.
- The water drains away and the new paper sheet is squeezed between two rollers.
- Making Paper
- Large papermaking machines can make up to 1,000 miles of paper a day.
- These are boiled in water and chemicals, and the resulting pulp is washed and pumped onto a moving wire screen.
- We use paper every day, but do we know how it is made?

The answer is in the **Answer Section** at the back of the book.

Writing skills The process paragraph (2)

Here are some pictures of a natural process: the life cycle of a frog. Make notes for a process paragraph, using the information in the pictures.

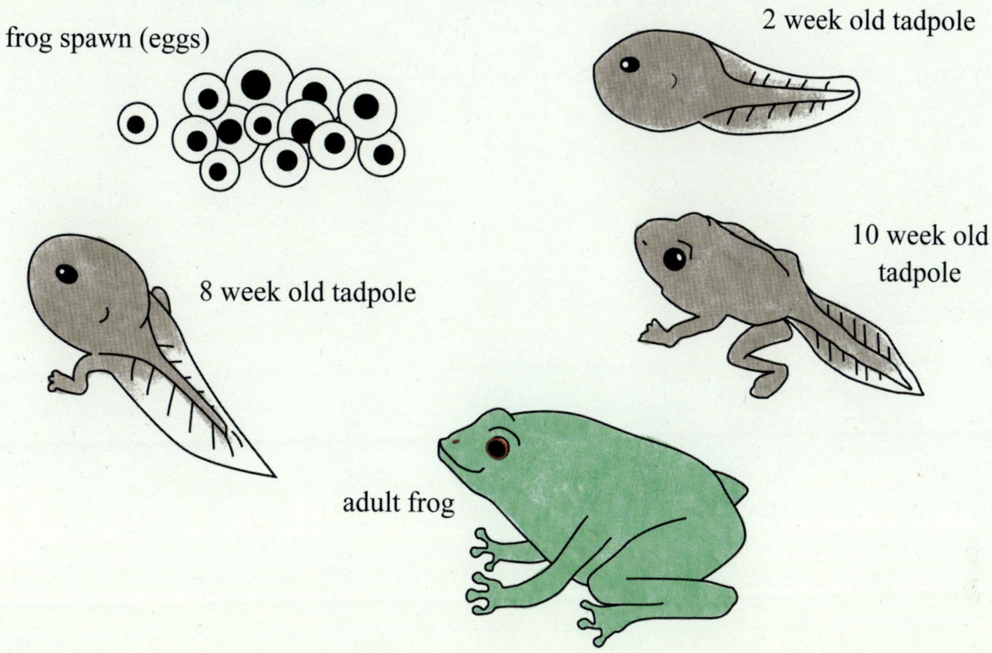

Title ____________________

Topic sentence ____________________

Body 1 ____________________

Body 2 ____________________

Body 3 ____________________

Body 4 ____________________

Conclusion ____________________

Don't forget the sequencing words (▸page 150):

first,	third,	then,	soon,	meanwhile,	Finally,
second,	next,	after that,	later,	the next step	

Check out the process paragraph links on the Unit 8 website ("Writing").

Writing practice *Brainstorming, outlining and first draft*

Choose a 'process' topic:

1. A natural process (animal/insect life cycles, the water cycle, thunder, typhoons, the seasons, or your choice.)
2. A man-made process (making steel, making yogurt, making videos, online shopping, or your choice.)

Brainstorm your ideas and put the process in sequence.

→ →

Now write your process paragraph.

Draft 1

Peer-editing

Exchange books with a classmate. Edit his/her first draft using the Checklist on page 95. Return the book and talk about your first drafts together.

Writing assignment Rewriting

Rewrite your paragraph, based on your classmate's editing and your own ideas.

Name: ____________________ Draft 2

____

____

____

____

____

____

____

____

____

____

____

Here is a checklist of things to look for when you are peer-editing. You should also use it for self-editing your second draft.

✓	Peer/Self-Editing Checklist	
☐	Capital letters	(**C** – pages 19 and 141)
☐	Punctuation	(**P** – pages 31 and 141)
☐	Apostrophes, personal pronouns	(**Gr1** - pages 44 and 141)
☐	Singular/plural, count/non-count	(**Gr2** - pages 55 and 141)
☐	Prepositions	(**Pr** – pages 79 and 141)
☐	Articles	(**Art** – pages 91 and 141)
☐	Paragraph format	(**Para** - pages 7 and 141)

Review corner *Self-assessment: Motivation*

How motivated are you to learn English? Rate your motivation in this chart.

3 = Very important; **2** = Quite important; **1** = Not important

	How important are these things to you?	1	2	3
1.	Having fun in English lessons			
2.	Feeling good about your English study			
3.	Being allowed to study English by yourself			
4.	Getting feedback about your work in English lessons			
5.	Speaking in English outside of class (foreigners, travel abroad)			
6.	Speaking in English in a test (University, job interview, TOEFL)			
7.	Speaking in English in your career (e-mail, reports)			
8.	Writing in English in a test (University, job, IELTS, etc.)			
9.	Writing in English in your career (e-mails, reports)			
10.	Listening to English outside of class (TV, Internet, movies)			
11.	Reading English outside of class (textbooks, newspapers)			
12.	Giving a presentation in English (University, career)			
	Total			

I need to improve my motivation in:

Review what you have done in this Unit and prepare for the next Unit.

Review
Browse the website for Unit 8.

Preview
Browse the website for Unit 9.

Prepare
Look at the activities in Unit 9.

Organize
Cut out this page and put it in the portfolio pocket.

http://www.finchpark.com/KNUFLE/

UNIT 9 Technology

My page — *Discoveries and inventions*

There have been many technological breakthroughs in history. Look at the pictures of groundbreaking technologies below and write their names in the boxes.

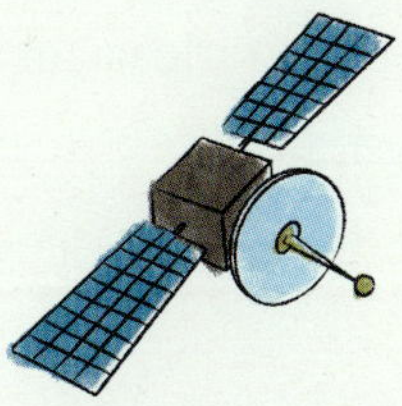

1.

2.

3.

4.

5.

6.

7.

8.

The answers are in the **Answer Section** at the back of the book.

Talk with a classmate about these technologies.

Which technology came first? Which came next?
Which ones can you live without? Why?
Which ones can you not live without? Why?
Can you think of any other technological discoveries or inventions?

> ***Today's quotation*:** "One machine can do the work of fifty ordinary men. No machine can do the work of one extraordinary man." (Elbert Hubbard)

Reading and discussing (step 1)

Track 37

Read this passage, find vocabulary, and then talk about the discussion topics.

Seasteading

It seems these days that more and more land is being used for cities, roads or factories. As a result, there is less and less land for growing food. Because of this, seasteading, also known as 'homesteading on the high seas,' aims to build floating communities. These sea-cities would grow their own food and make their own energy. They would also be outside national borders and could make their own laws. The idea might seem wild at first, but as more and more oil-rigs are being closed down, each of which could hold hundreds of condos, the idea of floating cities becomes more believable.

There are already some sea-based communities: 'Sealand' is a micro-nation off the east coast of England; pirate radio stations sail in international waters; furthermore, 'Women on Waves' offers help to women around the world. There are also ideas for converting cruise ships into seasteads. Who knows what the future might hold?

Vocabulary in context

Choose two or three unfamiliar words and write them in the table. Find the meanings (Glossary, ▸pages 151–168). Write a sentence for each word.

word	sentence
1	
2	
3	

Discussion topics

1. Would you like to live in a floating city? Explain your opinion.

2. What do you think homes will look like in the future?

3. Do you agree that "The ocean is the next frontier of human civilization"?
*http://www.seasteading.org
[Yes] Why? [No] Why not?

There are more reading passages at http://finchpark.com/KNUFLE/book-1/unit09/read.html.

Reading and discussing (step 2)

Track 38

Read this passage, find vocabulary, and then talk about the discussion topics.

Dress Smart

Clothes keep us warm in cold weather and cool in hot weather. They are also expressions of fashion. However, clothes of the future will have many new functions. They will probably adapt to different temperatures, protect us from UV-radiation, change color, monitor our heart rate, and connect us to the Internet. Imagine charging your cellular phone by plugging it into your shirt or your dress. Imagine clothes that contact your doctor when you are ill.

Believe it or not, scientists have made a fabric that looks like cotton, but conducts electricity. The cotton fibers in the material are coated with semiconductors, while small solar power cells store electricity which can be accessed through a USB connection.

This 'smart' material is a small taste of the new wearable technology. Scientists are becoming fashion experts with the creation and development of this ultra-cool material, and there is much more to come.

Vocabulary in context

Choose some unfamiliar words from the passage and write them below. Check the Glossary (▸ pages 151–168) for their meanings. Write a new sentence for each word.

word	sentence
1	
2	
3	

Discussion topics

1. Would you like to wear smart clothes? [Yes] Why? [No] Why not?

2. What will clothes look like in the future?

3. Can scientists be good fashion designers? Explain your opinion.

There are more reading passages at http://www.finchpark.com/KNUFLE/book-1/unit09/read.html.

Reading and discussing (step 3)

Track 39

Read this passage, find vocabulary, and then discuss the topics on the next page.

Technology for Change

There is a saying that yesterday's Science Fiction is today's reality. This is certainly true for the TV series, *Star Trek*, which stunned viewers nearly 50 years ago with its futuristic technology. Since then it has given birth to movies, novels and computer/video games. There is even an online *Star Trek* encyclopedia, called *Memory Alpha*. Just like Captain Kirk of the Starship Enterprise, we now have satellite communication, e-mail, chat rooms and video-conferencing. We can access huge databases of information on the Internet and smart technologies are making our lives more comfortable.

However, technology is not just about making luxury gadgets. Medicine is also benefitting from hi-tech developments in optics, surgery, cancer treatment and other fields. Technology can also help people in countries where poverty is a reality. For example, the nonprofit organization One Laptop Per Child aims to give a computer to every child in the developing world. This will help them to get an education, even if they can't go to school, so that they can gain skills and knowledge to help their country in the future.

The creator, producer, and writer of *Star Trek*, Gene Roddenberry, told friends that Jonathan Swift's novel *Gulliver's Travels* was his model. He wanted each episode to be a morality tale as well as an adventure story, and he wanted to show how mankind might progress if it could learn from the past. Because of this, each episode of Star Trek looked at human issues that recur throughout history.

Roddenberry wanted science and ethics to work together to improve everybody's lives. Let's hope that his dream comes true.

Vocabulary in context

Choose three unfamiliar words from this passage and write them below. Look in the Glossary (▸pages 151–168) to find the meanings and write a sentence for each word.

word	sentence
1	
2	
3	

There are more reading passages at http://www.finchpark.com/KNUFLE/book-1/unit09/read.html.

Discussion topics

Discuss these questions about the reading text (▸page 100) together.

1. Do you like Sci-Fi movies? [Yes] Why? [No] Why not?
2. Would you like to work in a non-profit organization? Why? Why not?
3. How can technology help people in underdeveloped countries?
4. Do you know any stories like *Gulliver's Travels*? Talk about them.
5. How can science and ethics work together?

Here are some Science Fiction stories about time travel:

In *A Sound of Thunder*, Ray Bradbury tells of the year 2055. The main character goes back in time to hunt dinosaurs. However, he is scared and steps off the path, treading on a butterfly. When he returns to the present, he finds that many things have changed because of the death of the butterfly.

In the South Korean movie *2009: Lost Memories*, Japan won WWII and Korea is a Japanese colony. The heroes go back in time and change history. Because of them, Korea is as it is today.

Finally, in *Time's Arrow*, by Arthur C. Clarke, two geologists find dinosaur footprints. Meanwhile, scientists in a nearby laboratory have made a liquid that takes them back in time. However, their jeep explodes and the geologists discover the jeep's tire tracks next to the dinosaur footprints. Millions of years ago, the dinosaur changed direction to miss the jeep.

- Do you think time travel is possible?
- If you could travel back in time, which period of history would you visit? Why?

Interacting *What if?*

Look at the board game on this page. Roll the dice and move your marker. What topic have you landed on? Talk about it for 30 seconds.

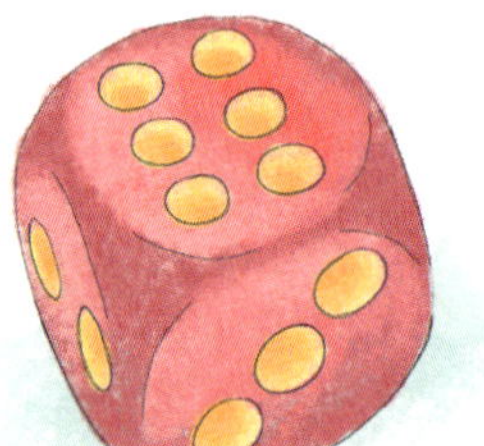

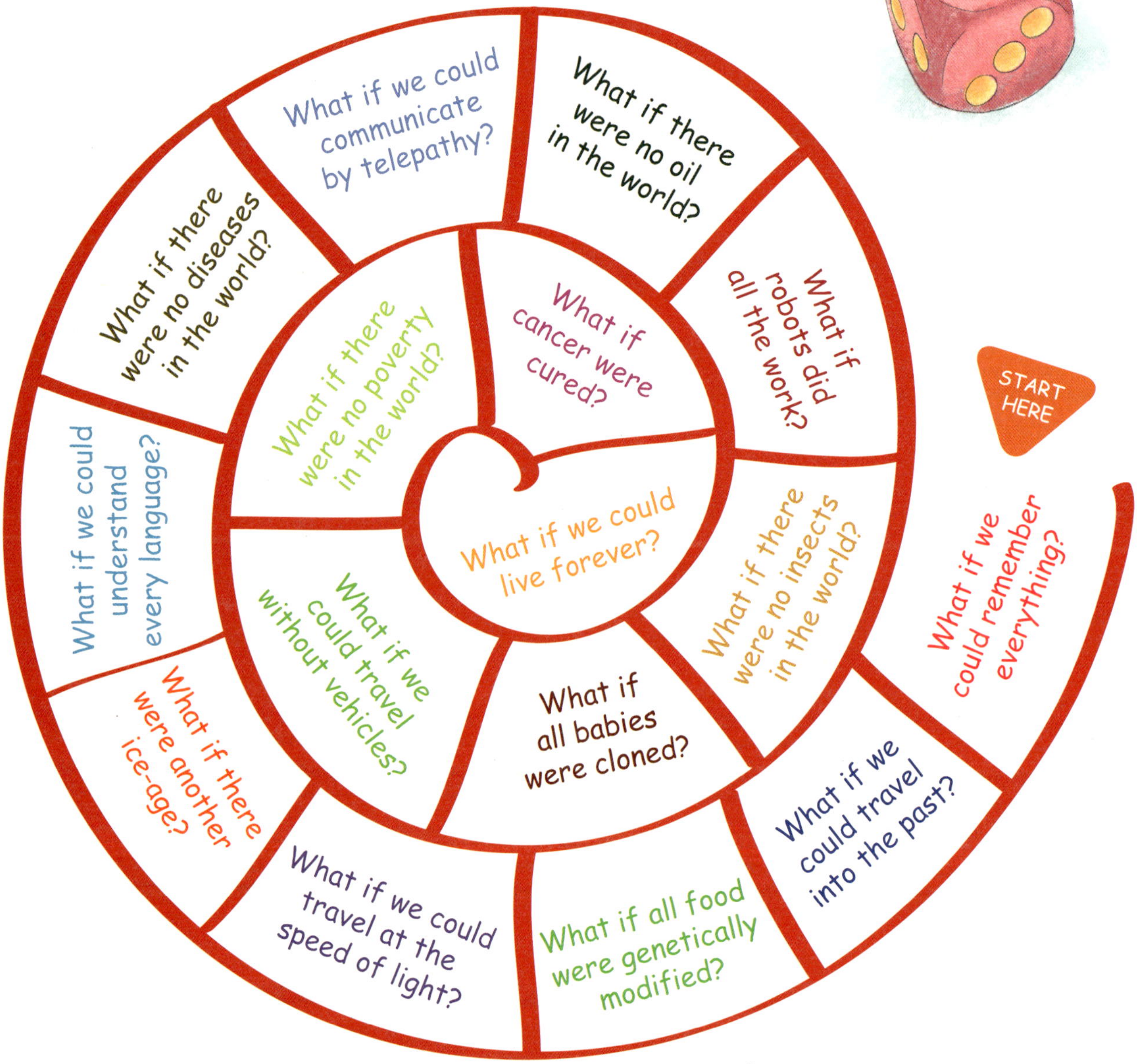

How about making your own rules for the game?

Our rules:

1. ______________________________

2. ______________________________

3. ______________________________

Writing workshop *Consistency (Subject/verb)*

Talk about the following sentences and make corrections where necessary.

1. The soccer team practice in the gym every day.

____

2. Most people likes to see a good movie.

____

3. He doesn't likes horror movies.

____

4. Mary and her friends has gone shopping.

____

5. One of the books have disappeared.

____

Read the paragraph below and edit it for Subject/verb agreement (**S/v**).

The Advantages and Disadvantages of Fast Food

I likes (S/v → like) fast food because it are (S/v → is) very convenient. The main advantage are (S/v → is) that it save time. I can eats immediately at fast food restaurants, whereas when I cooks at home I have to buys the ingredients, prepares them, and cooks the meal. Another advantage are that fast foods like burgers and fries is quite cheap, while others, like salads and whole-grain bread rolls, is also healthy.

However, there is also disadvantages. Fast food contain more salt, fats and calories than home-cooked meals. Because of this, it can causes obesity. In addition, many families spends less time eating together. We needs to thinks about the pros and cons of fast food and makes sure we eats a balanced diet.

The answers for this Writing Workshop page are in the **Answer Section**, at the back of the book.
There are more subject/verb agreement activities on the website for Unit 9 ("Writing").

Thinking skills Double meanings (problem-solving)

When we write a paragraph, the title is very important. Here are some confusing newspaper headlines. Can you improve them?

GLOBAL VILLAGE TALKS TODAY	arms company has new head	SCHOLARSHIP STUDENTS DEMAND LOWER TUITION FEES
FORGOTTEN WAR HEROES REMEMBERED	magician faints during hot spell	DUMB WITNESS SPEAKS OUT
Plans for new skating rink put on ice	GOVERNMENT ACTS ON THEATRE LAW	MINISTER CALLS FOR MORE SPELLING TESTS IN SKOOLS
House prices go through the roof	POLICE LOOKING FOR INVISIBLE MAN	NEW CERAMIC KNIVES USE CUTTING EDGE TECHNOLOGY
ROBBER TAKES STOLEN PAINTING	AIR FARES TAKE OFF	Bodies of crash survivors flown home

Writing skills Advantages and disadvantages paragraphs

These are like listing paragraphs (▸Unit 2) and comparison paragraphs (▸Unit 5). They list the advantages and disadvantages, then they compare them. Here is a two-paragraph sample.

Track 40

The Advantages and Disadvantages of Technology

On the one hand, it is hard to imagine living without technology, since there are many advantages. For example, cars and planes make it possible to travel in comfort, smart phones let us communicate with people anywhere, and robots and machines do things quicker and better than humans. In addition, computers give us speedy access to information. These technologies make life easier and save time.

On the other hand, technology also has disadvantages. The use of machines and robots leads to fewer jobs, pollution produces global warming, computers crash, and roads become blocked with heavy traffic. Besides, new diseases such as obesity are appearing. In view of these facts, we need to weigh the advantages and disadvantages of technology carefully and ask the question: "Has technology brought happiness or a more stressful lifestyle?"

These mind maps and outlines show how the sample paragraphs were made.

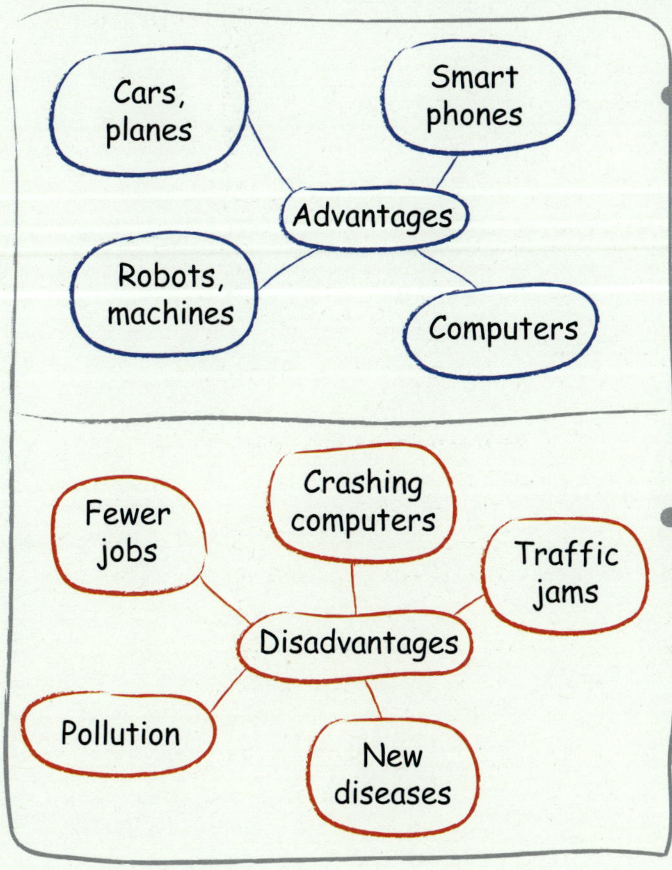

Paragraph 1
Topic sentence: advantages
Example 1: travel
Example 2: communication
Example 3: machines
Example 4: computers
Conclusion sentence: convenience

Paragraph 2
Topic sentence: disadvantages
Example 1: fewer jobs
Example 2: pollution
Example 3: computer problems
Example 4: traffic jams
Example 5: new diseases
Conclusion sentence: comparison

Writing practice *Brainstorming, outlining and first draft*

First of all, choose a topic for your advantages/disadvantages two-paragraph essay. Here are some ideas:

1. The Internet
2. Living alone
3. Television
4. Living in a city
5. Study groups
6. Globalization
7. ____________ (Your idea)

Now brainstorm your ideas and make an outline (▸page 105).

Advantages	→ Paragraph 1
Disadvantages	→ Paragraph 2

Next, write your 2-paragraph essay. Use the 'Advantages and Disadvantages' words on the next page (See also ▸page 144).

____________ Draft 1

Peer-editing

Exchange books with a classmate and edit his/her 1st draft (▸page 106) using the Marking Code and the Paragraph Checklist on page 141. Return the book and talk about your first drafts together.

Writing assignment Rewriting

Rewrite your paragraph, based on this editing and on your own ideas.

Name: ______________________ Final draft

____

____

____

____

____

____

____

____

____

____

____

____

____

Here are some phrases you can use (▸page 144):

On the one hand,	The positive side of it is that …	Another thing is that …
On the other hand,	The negative aspect of it is …	I'm afraid to say that …
One advantage is that …	The problem is …	The main advantage is that …
One disadvantage is that …	One drawback is that …	The main disadvantage is that …

Review corner — *Self-assessment: Emotional management*

Find out about your emotional intelligence in the following chart.

3 = Very well; **2** = So-so; **1** = Not well

	Answer these questions:	**3**	**2**	**1**
1.	How well do I understand myself?			
2.	How well do I understand my learning needs?			
3.	How well do I understand other people?			
4.	How well do I manage my emotions?			
5.	How well do I deal with others and their problems?			
6.	How well do I deal with changing situations?			
7.	How well do I deal with stress before a test?			
8.	How well do I deal with assignments and deadlines?			
9.	How well do I deal with nervousness and anxiety?			
10.	How well do I inspire myself to improve and work hard?			
11.	How well do I inspire others to work hard and do their best?			
12.	How well do I create a positive environment around me?			
	Total			

I need to improve my emotional management in terms of:

Now review what you have done in this Unit and prepare for the next Unit.

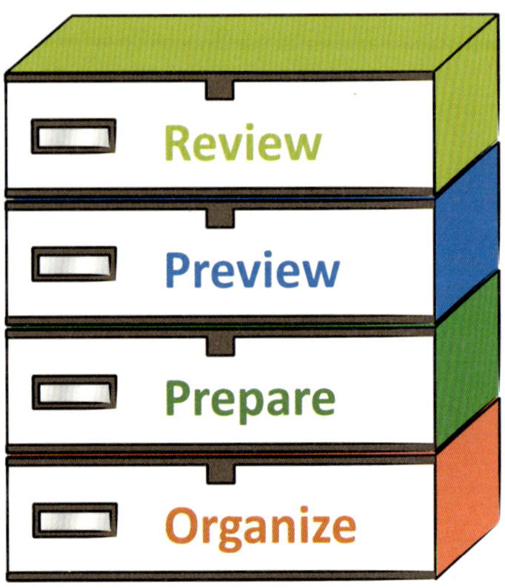

- Browse the website for Unit 9.
- Browse the website for Unit 10.
- Look at the activities in Unit 10.
- Cut out this page and put it in the portfolio pocket.

http://www.finchpark.com/KNUFLE/book-1/index.html

UNIT 10

Renewable energy

My page Energy types

Here are some energy types. Some of them are renewable (sustainable) and some of them are non-renewable. What do you know about these types?

BIOMASS *renewable*

HYDROPOWER *renewable*

GEOTHERMAL *renewable*

SOLAR *renewable*

PETROLEUM *non-renewable*

NATURAL GAS *non-renewable*

COAL *non-renewable*

URANIUM *non-renewable*

WIND *renewable*

What are the advantages (pros) and disadvantages (cons) of the different energy types? Write your ideas in the table below.

	Pros:	Cons:
Non-renewable energy		
Renewable energy		

Talk about energy types with a classmate. Try to persuade him/her to agree with you.

Today's quotation: "Practically every environmental problem we have can be traced to our addiction to fossil fuels, primarily oil." (Dennis Weaver)

2012 was the UN International Year of Sustainable Energy for All.

Reading and discussing (step 1)

Track 41

Read this passage, find vocabulary, and then talk about the discussion topics.

Green Korea

Did you know that the village of Donggwang in Seogwipo City, Jeju Island, gets 100 percent of its power from the sun? All the houses and the local school have solar panels on their roofs. Jeju Island also has a large wind farm, which will provide 20 percent of the island's electricity by 2020.

Like other Asian countries, Korea is developing clean and green energy. The 'Green Korea' plan lists nine areas for investment, including solar power, wind power, light-emitting diodes, hydrogen fuel cells, and energy storage. The world's largest solar plant opened in Shinan in 2008, making enough electricity for 10,000 homes, and a huge offshore wind farm is being built on the west coast.

There are already solar-powered mobile phones on sale, and the government is encouraging next-generation car engines, which can use different types of fuels, including natural gas. Alternative energy is big business in Korea, and the government predicts a need for 1 million green jobs by 2030.

Vocabulary in context

Choose two or three unfamiliar words and write them in the table. Find the meanings (Glossary, ▸pages 151–168). Write a sentence for each word.

word	sentence
1	
2	
3	

Discussion topics

1. Would you like to use solar energy in your house? [Yes] Why? [No] Why not?

2. Would you like a green job? [Yes] What sort of job? [No] Why not?

3. How can you help Korea become clean and green?

There are more reading passages at http://www.finchpark.com/KNUFLE/book-1/unit10/read.html.

Reading and discussing (step 2)

Track 42

Read this passage, find vocabulary, and then talk about the discussion topics.

A Greener World

Modern economies use petroleum in every walk of life. However, oil is getting expensive and will eventually run out. In contrast, renewable energy comes from clean fuels, which do not harm the environment and which are naturally renewed.

As well as hydropower, solar energy, wind power, geothermal energy, and biomass energy, there are many other clean energy sources. For example, green speed bumps generate power as cars drive over them, producing electricity for streetlights, traffic lights, and road signs. A nightclub in the Netherlands gets energy from people dancing on the dance floor. Other sources such as beer, onions, spinach, farm waste, salt, watermelons, bugs, viruses, and landfills, produce methane gas, which can be used to generate electricity. Scientists are also making trees with artificial leaves. These will make clean fuels from sunlight and wind. They are even talking about solar power from outer space. If renewable energy can satisfy world energy needs, perhaps we can hope for a greener, cleaner future.

Vocabulary in context

Choose some unfamiliar words from the passage and write them below. Check the Glossary (▸pages 151–168) for their meanings. Write a new sentence for each word.

word	sentence
1	
2	
3	

Discussion topics

1. How will our lives change when there is no more oil?

2. What are 'clean fuels'? Why are they called 'clean'?

3. Can clean fuels provide all our energy? Explain your opinion.

There are more reading passages at http://www.finchpark.com/KNUFLE/book-1/unit10/read.html.

Reading and discussing (step 3)

Track 43

Read this passage, find vocabulary, and then discuss the topics on the next page.

Global Warming

Christmas Day 2011 was the warmest day on record at the South Pole, with a temperature of 9.9° Fahrenheit (–12.3° Celsius). In 2009, the average temperature for the whole year was –47.9°C, making it the warmest year since records began in 1957. This was unfortunate for people wanting to join the '300 Club,' since the rules of the club state that the temperature must reach –100° F (–73°C). Would-be members then warm up in a 200° F (93°C) sauna and rush outside, experiencing a 300-degree temperature difference. They run to the pole that marks the geographic South Pole and then run back into the sauna to get warm.

According to the National Oceanic and Atmospheric Administration (NOAA) 2009 was the fourth warmest year since global records began in 1895. The hottest year was the 12 months up to July 2012, followed by 2010 and 2005. In addition, the last 15 years have included 13 of the warmest years on record. These high temperatures have caused the polar icecaps and glaciers around the world to melt even faster, increasing the possibility of avalanches, landslides, and floods. Scientists point out that as the ice melts, the pressure on the earth's crust lessens. This can affect earthquake faults and even set off volcanoes. When the last ice age ended, 12,000 to 15,000 years ago, there was a jump in volcanic activity of 300 percent.

The American Association for the Advancement of Science (AAAS) made an official statement on climate change in 2006:

> *The scientific evidence is clear: global climate change caused by human activities is occurring now, and it is a growing threat to society. The time to control greenhouse gas emissions is now.* (http://www.aaas.org)

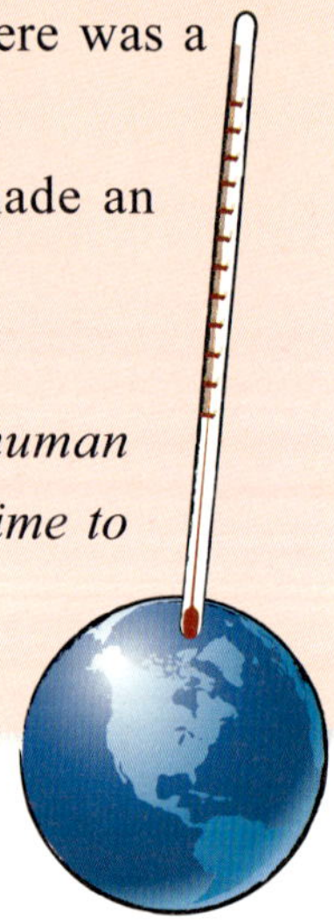

Vocabulary in context

Choose some unfamiliar words from this passage and write them below. Look in the Glossary (▸pages 151–168) for their meanings. Write a new sentence for each word.

word	sentence
1	
2	
3	

There are more reading passages at http://www.finchpark.com/KNUFLE/book-1/unit10/read.html.

Discussion topics

Think about the reading text (▸page 112) and discuss these questions.

1. Would you like to join the '300 Club'? [Yes] Why? [No] Why not?

2. Would you like to visit the South Pole? [Yes] Why? [No] Why not?

3. Have you noticed climate change in your life? Talk about your experience.

4. Have you seen any movies about climate change? What did you think of them?

5. What can we do about global warming and climate change?

Many products that we use every day are made from coal and oil. Can you live without them for one day? One week? One month? One year? Forever? Discuss these products. Which ones are absolutely necessary?

ballpoint pens
batteries
billiard balls
bowling balls
cameras
carpets
combs
crayons
credit cards
deodorant
detergents
eyeglasses
fertilizer
footballs
glue
golf balls
guitar strings
hair coloring
hand lotion
lipstick
medicines
nail polish
nylon rope
paint
paper clips
parachutes
perfumes
pesticides
pillows
plastic
rubber bands
shampoo
shoes
soda water
soft lenses
sugar substitute
sunglasses
telephones
tennis rackets
tires
toothbrushes
toothpaste
trash bags
umbrellas

 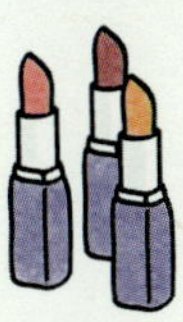 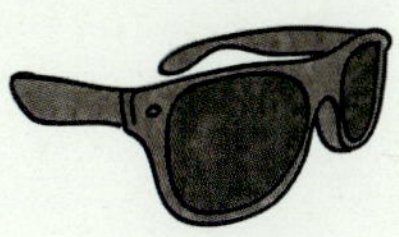 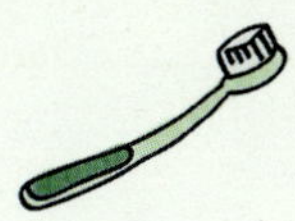 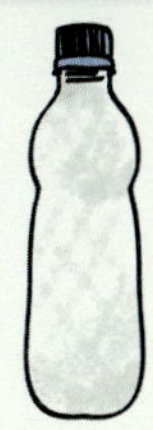

Interacting *Energy Quiz Show*

Make a quiz show about renewable energy.

1. Choose one person to be the MC. The MC's question cards are on page 143.
2. Take turns to choose a box: *I'll have Solar energy for 10 points, please.*
3. Answer the MC's questions.
4. Write your score at the bottom of the page.

Hydro energy	Solar energy	Biomass energy	Geothermal energy	Wind energy
Water 5 points	Solar 5 points	Biomass 5 points	Geo 5 points	Wind 5 points
Water 10 points	Solar 10 points	Biomass 10 points	Geo 10 points	Wind 10 points
Water 15 points	Solar 15 points	Biomass 15 points	Geo 15 points	Wind 15 points
Water 20 points	Solar 20 points	Biomass 20 points	Geo 20 points	Wind 20 points

My Score:

Writing workshop Word order

Talk about the following sentences and write them correctly. There are more 'word order' activities on the website for Unit 10 ("Writing").

1. Does she every week play table tennis?
   WO
   Does she play table tennis every week?
2. We're going on Tuesday to visit her.
   ____
3. For a long time they were married.
   ____
4. I want really to speak well English.
   ____
5. Jeremy walks always to school.
   ____
6. She is only the person who can this puzzle solve.
   ____

The answers are in the **Answer Section**, at the back of the book.

There is an order for adjectives when we use more than one in a sentence.

1 number		2 opinion	3 size	4 shape	5 color	6 age	7 origin	8 material
first	one	nice	big	round	white	young	Italian	leather
second	two	warm	small	square	red	old	German	plastic
third	three	beautiful	long	oval	yellow	ancient	Brazilian	wool

Let's play a game using this order. (Make your own sentences.)

Step 1: A group member starts a sentence: "This is my hat."

Step 2: The next person adds an adjective: "This is my second hat."

Step 3: The next person adds an adjective: "This is my second cute hat."

Step 4: The next person adds an adjective: "This is my second cute big hat."

Step 5: ....

Step 6: ....

Step 7: ....

Step 8: ....

Writing skills *Cause and effect paragraphs (1)*

Cause and effect paragraphs tell us what happened (the effect) and why it happened (the cause). Here is a sequence of events. Talk about these events together.

We can turn these events into a cause and effect paragraph by: Track 44

❶ adding a topic sentence,
❷ using the 'cause and effect' words in the Word Bank (▸page 146),
❸ adding a conclusion sentence.

The Final Exam

I was having trouble balancing work and play during the semester and I didn't study at all. At last, the final exam was the next day. For this reason, I studied till 3 am the night before the exam, with the result that I overslept the next morning. Hence I couldn't get ready in time, so that I missed the bus. Due to this, I was late for the exam. Because of this, my grade was terrible. Consequently, I have learned a lesson and have decided that I must manage my time better in future.

There is more information about cause and effect paragraphs on the website for this Unit ("Writing").

Writing skills *Cause and effect paragraphs (2)*

Actions (causes) lead to results (effects), which often cause more results. Here are some more sequences. How do you think they are linked?

Clean energy	Water not safe to drink	Crossing of national borders
Factory waste in rivers	Machines in factories	Farmworkers move to cities
Fossil fuels →	No pollution	Fishes and plants die
Increasing population	More roads and cities	Global warming
Industrial Revolution	→ Pollution →	Improved lifestyle
Smart technology	Increased communication	Less land for food
The Internet	Access to information	No climate change

Use the picture below and the 'Hints' to the right of the picture to tell the fortune of a classmate. Then write your predictions at the bottom of the page. Use the 'Cause and effect' words on page 119.

1: Heart Line
2: Head Line
3: Life Line
4: Fate Line
5: Marriage Line
6: Travel Line
7: Fame Line

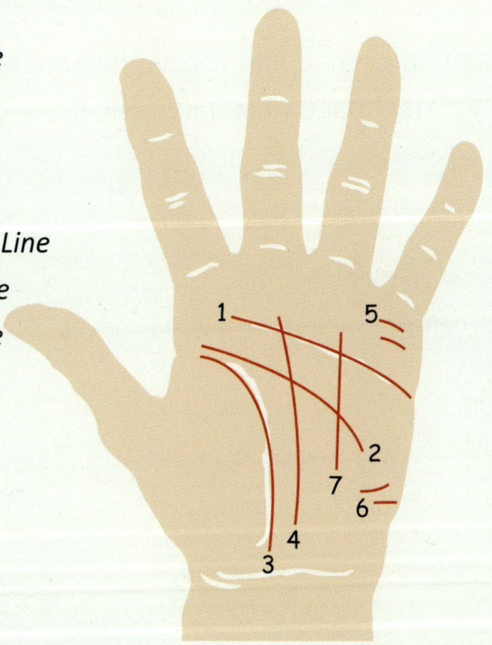

Hints

be healthy	travel abroad
be very lucky	run a business
become famous	pass your exams
become rich	make new friends
build a house	follow your dream
find a partner	be very happy
get married	be successful
go to Australia	be intelligent
have a family	be a soccer star
live long	be a singer
study hard	achieve your goals

You have a strong marriage line,	→	so you will find a great partner,	→	and as a result, you will be very happy.
	→		→	
	→		→	
	→		→	
	→		→	

Writing practice *Brainstorming, outlining and first draft*

You are going to write an e-mail to the President of Korea, about an issue that is important to you. Choose a topic for your e-mail.

1. University tuition fees
2. Shortage of jobs
3. Renewable energy
4. Low birth rate
5. .... (Your own topic)

Now brainstorm the causes and effects that you are going to write about.

Causes	→	Effects

Write your first draft. Use the 5 parts of an e-mail and formal language (Unit 1), and the 'Cause and effect' words on the next page (also page 146).

Draft 1

To

Subject

Attach a file Receipt On Read : Receipt On Delivery :

Cc Bcc Signature Addresses Save Draft Send Check Spelling

Peer-editing

Exchange books with a classmate. Edit his/her first draft using the Marking Code and the Paragraph Checklist on page 141. Return the book and talk about your first drafts together.

Writing assignment *Rewriting*

Rewrite your e-mail, based on your classmate's editing and on your own ideas. Use the 'cause and effect' words at the bottom of the page.

To ______

Subject ______

Name: ______

Attach a file | Receipt On Read : ☐ | Receipt On Delivery : ☐

Cc | Bcc | Signature | Addresses | Save Draft | Send | Check Spelling

Draft 2

______

______

______

______

______

______

______

______

______

______

______

______

______

Cause and effect words

So,	Due to …	Therefore,	Otherwise,	For this reason,
Thus,	Since …	Wherefore	Thereupon	For these reasons,
Hence,	So that …	Accordingly,	Consequently,	For this purpose,
Then …	Because …	As a result,	Subsequently,	With the result that …

Review corner *Self-assessment: Social awareness*

Do you know the goals of education in Korea?

> *The objectives of education, under the ideals of Hongik-Ingan, the founding philosophy of Korea, are to help all people perfect their individual characters, develop the self-sustaining ability to attain independent lives, acquire the qualifications of democratic citizens, participate in the makings of a democratic state, and promote the prosperity of all humankind. (http://www.ibe.unesco.org)*

How will you contribute to society and humanity? Write about your social awareness below. There are some useful words in the **Word Bank**, on pages 140 (Social awareness) and 150 (Wants, needs and wishes).

My social awareness	
Environment	
Art and Culture	
Citizenship	
Current Affairs	
Values	

Now review what you have done in this Unit and prepare for the next Unit.

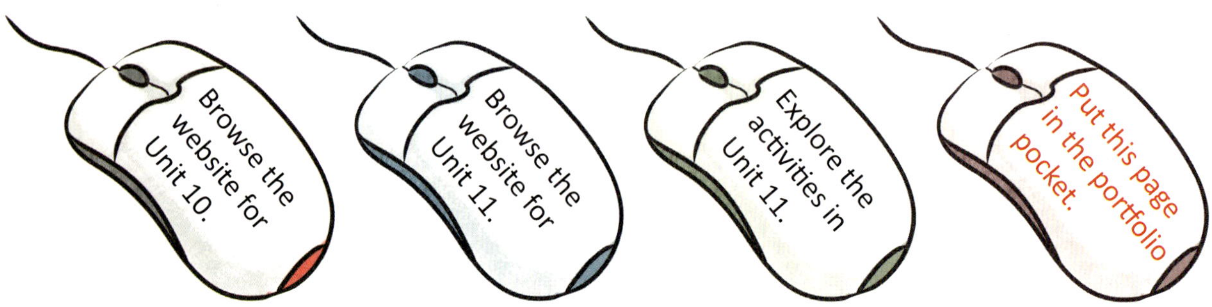

www.finchpark.com/KNUFLE/book-1/

UNIT 11 Presentations

My page *My presentation skills*

Look at the questions below and answer them based on your experience.

1. Have you ever seen a presentation in English?	Yes	No
2. Have you ever given a presentation?	Yes	No
3. Will you have to give presentations in your department?	Yes	No
4. Will you have to give presentations in your future career?	Yes	No

5. What makes a good presentation?
6. What makes a bad presentation?
7. How should the presenter speak?
8. How should the presenter dress?
9. Do you know any presentation "Dos"?
10. Do you know any presentation "Don'ts"?

Talk to a classmate about your answers.

What do you think makes a good presentation?
Do you know any presentation "Dos" and "Don'ts"?

Today's quotation: "It takes one hour of preparation for each minute of presentation time." (Wayne Burgraff)

Presentations *Choosing a topic*

Your group will give a presentation in a few weeks, so you need to choose your topic. Here are some suggestions. You can also choose your own topic.

1 Make a presentation about a festival or a national holiday. Find interesting data about the festival (history, location, time of year, events, symbolism). ▶ (Unit 5)

2 Make a presentation about a myth or a legend. Find interesting data (origin, different versions, symbolism, meaning, application to modern life, etc). ▶ (Unit 6)

3 Make a presentation about healthy food (benefits, medicinal value, anti-cancer, fermented food, etc.). You could choose one food, or talk about healthy food in general. ▶ (Unit 7)

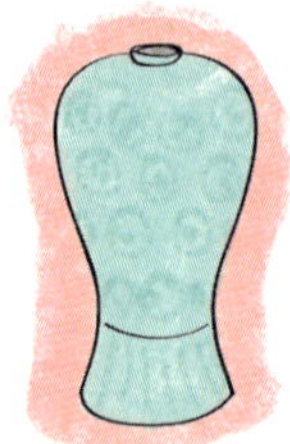

4 Make a presentation about culture and diversity. You could choose one culture or talk about various cultures. Think about customs, art, music, dancing, food, beliefs, etc. ▶ (Unit 8)

5 Make a presentation about smart technology. What are the latest developments? How is technology changing our lives? How is it affecting traditions, cultures, quality of life, education, jobs, beliefs, behavior, etc.? ▶ (Unit 9)

6 Make a presentation about how personal actions can affect the environment (recycling, consumer awareness, public transport, water conservation, etc.). ▶ (Unit 10)

Choose a topic for your group and write it in the box below. If you cannot decide right now, write the topic here as soon as you can.

Our topic:

Presentation skills (1) *Structure*

Presentations follow a basic structure.

Step	Stage	Tasks
1	Introduction	1. Welcome the audience and introduce yourself. 2. Introduce the topic of the presentation.
2	Outline	3. Give a brief outline of the presentation. 4. Tell the audience when they can ask questions.
3	Main Part	5. Start and finish sections clearly. 6. Analyze points and give examples. 7. Paraphrase and clarify.
4	Summary	8. Signal the end clearly. 9. Summarize the main points.
5	Conclusion	10. Close (short and simple).
6	Q & A	11. Invite questions. 12. Clarify the questions and answer politely.

Language focus 1 *Introduction*

Track 45

1. Welcome the audience and introduce yourself.

- Good afternoon (morning) everyone (ladies and gentlemen).
- Thank you for coming to this presentation today.
- My name is … … … and I'm a freshman/sophomore/junior/senior studying at Kyungpook National University, majoring in … … …

2. Introduce the topic of the presentation.

- Today, I am going (would like) to talk about … … …
- In this presentation, I will explain … … …
- The topic today is … … …
- The purpose of this presentation is … … …
- My presentation will take about …… minutes.
- I hope you will find the presentation interesting.

Language focus 2 *Outline*

Track 46

3. Give a brief outline of the presentation.

- I have divided my talk into four parts.
- My presentation is in four parts.
- I'd like to make a number of points.
- Briefly, I have three things to say.
- Firstly (First of all), I will talk about … … …
- Secondly (And then), I will move on to … … …
- Thirdly (Next), I will show that … … …
- Finally (Lastly) I'd like to finish by saying … … …

4. Tell the audience when they can ask questions.

- I'll be happy to answer questions at the end of the presentation.
- Please save your questions for the Q & A session at the end.
- There will be time for questions at the end.
- Feel free to interrupt if you have any questions.

Language focus 3 *Main part*

Track 47

5. Start and finish sections clearly.

- Moving on to … … …,
- The next issue (topic) I'd like to focus on is … … …
- Now let's move on to … … …
- Let's look at the next item now.
- I'd like to look at … … …

6. Analyze points and give examples.

- Let's consider this more carefully.
- What does this mean for … … … ?
- The significance of this is … … …
- As an illustration, … … …
- To illustrate this point, … … …
- Why is this important?
- A good example of this is … … …
- To give you an example, … … …

7. Paraphrase and clarify.

- Simply put, … … …
- In other words, … … …
- So what I'm saying is … … …
- Let's consider this in more detail.
- To put it more simply … … …
- To put it another way, … … …

Language focus 4 Summary

Track 48

8. Signal the end clearly.

- This brings me to the end of my presentation.

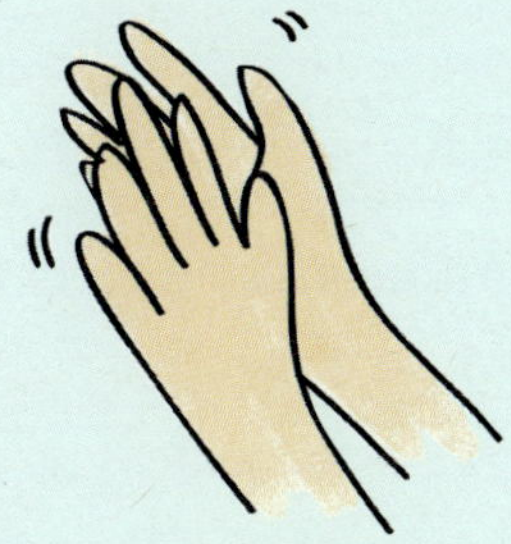

9. Summarize the main points.

- Let's look at what I've been saying.
- If I can just sum up the main points, ...
- Finally, let me remind you of the main points.
- To remind you of what I've covered in this talk, ...
- To sum up, ... / In conclusion, ... / My conclusion is that ... ...
- I've run out of time, so I'll conclude by saying that ... ...

Language focus 5 Conclusion

Track 49

No-one ever complains about a speech being too short. (Ira Hayes)

10. Close (short and simple).

- Thank you for listening.
- Thank you for your attention.

Language focus 6 Question time

Track 50

11. Invite questions.

- Now, I'd like to invite questions or comments.
- Does anyone have any questions or comments?
- Are there any questions?
- Would you like to ask any questions?

12. Clarify the questions and answer politely.

- If I understand you correctly, you are saying that ... ...
- I didn't quite catch that. Could you say it again?
- I'm not sure if I understand your question. Could you rephrase it?
- Thank you for that question.
- I'm glad you asked that question.
- That's a very good question.

Presentation skills (2) *Four stages*

There are four stages in giving a presentation.
Here are some basic hints for each stage.

☐ Stage 1: Planning

1. Ask questions about the topic.
2. Make a title.
3. Brainstorm ideas on the topic.
4. Make a list of the points you want to cover.
5. Assign roles and duties to group members.

☐ Stage 2: Preparing

1. Keep It Short and Simple (KISS).
2. Make it clear and relevant.
3. Prepare, prepare, prepare.
4. Think about the audience.

If you fail to prepare, you are prepared to fail.(Anonymous)

☐ Stage 3: Practicing

1. Go through your part of the presentation by yourself. Time yourself.
2. Get a friend or family member to watch you and give advice.
3. Think about your spoken language (volume, pronunciation, intonation, speed).
4. Record your voice and listen to it.
5. Think about your body language (eye contact, facial expression, hands, body posture).
6. Practice in front of a mirror and watch your body language.

☐ Stage 4: Presenting

1. Get to the presentation site early.
2. Check the equipment before you start.
3. Give the handouts out before you start.
4. Begin on time.
5. Speak clearly and concisely.
6. Look confident and smile.
7. Finish on time, or a few minutes early.

There are always three speeches for every one you actually gave: the one you practiced, the one you gave, and the one you wish you had given. (Dale Carnegie)

Check out the links on the website for this Unit.

Stage 1: Planning

Have you chosen a topic (▸page 122)?
Use this page for planning your presentation.

- Ask questions about the topic (page 126).

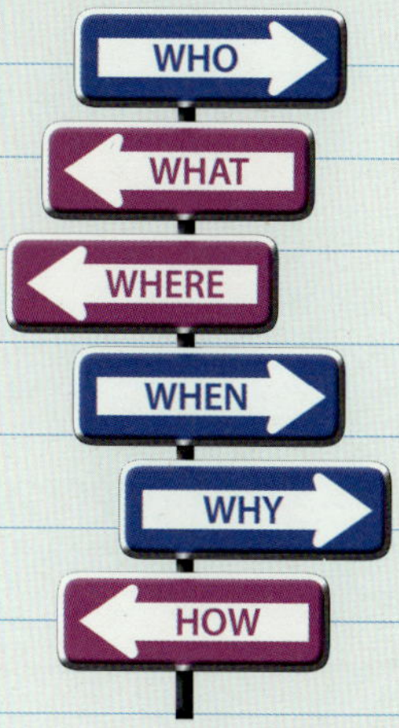

- Make a title.

- Brainstorm ideas on the topic.

- Make a list of ideas that you want to cover.

- Assign roles to group members.

Check out the links on the website for this Unit.

Stage 2: Preparing

Have you finished planning?
Use this page for preparing your part (▶page 126).

Plan | Prepare | Practice | Present

- My role in the presentation:

- I need to prepare these things:

- Here are my notes for the presentation:

Stage 3: Practicing

Use this page for writing and practicing your speech.

Plan Prepare Practice Present

- Here is my text for the presentation:

Stage 4: Presenting

Dos and Don'ts

It's time to give the presentation. However, before you get started, see if you can fill in the missing letters below and decide whether the tips from 1 to 19 are Dos (✓) or Don'ts (✗).

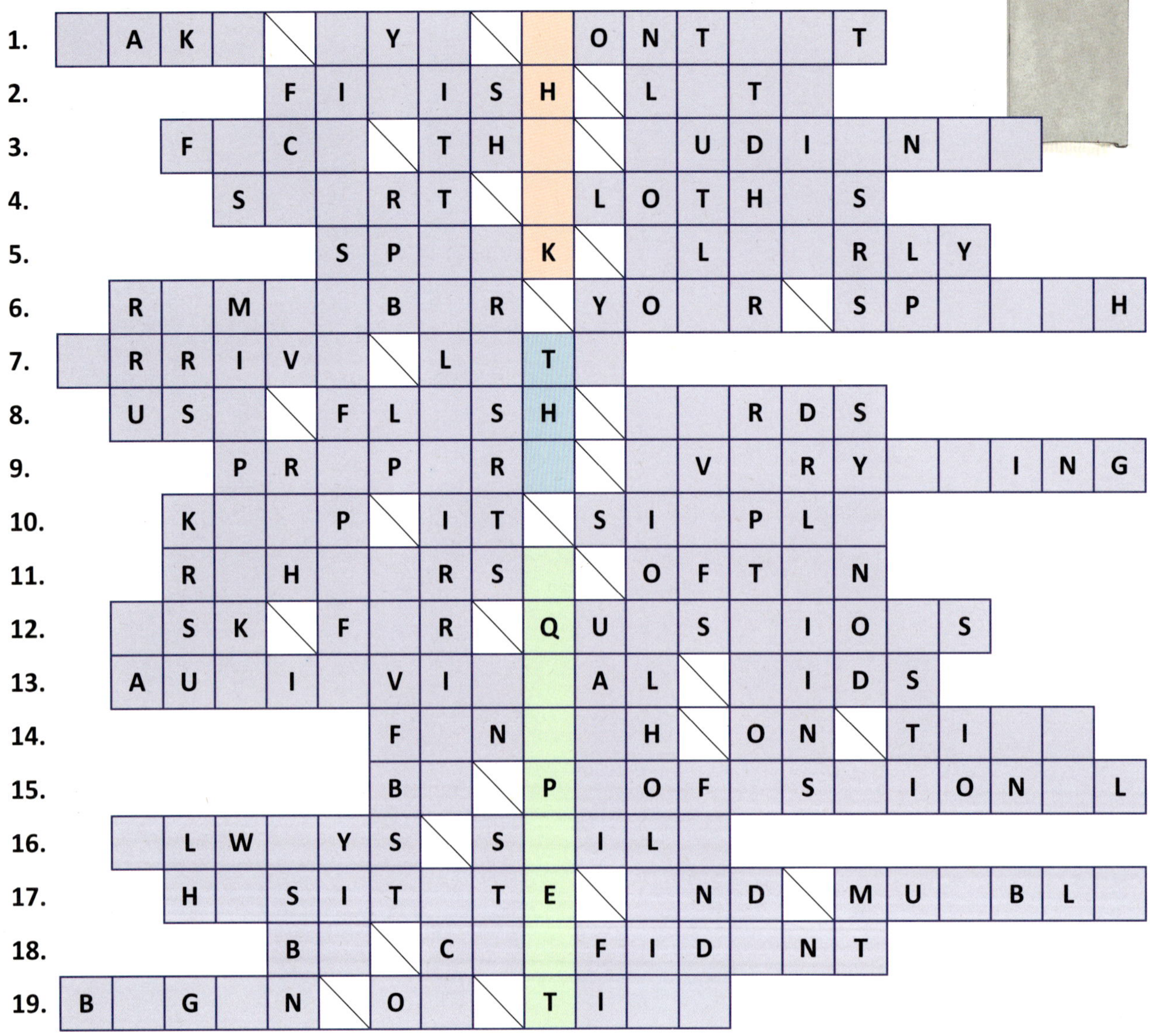

This puzzle is based on pages 61 and 62 of *It's Up to You!*, Finch and Sampson (2004).

1	2	3	4	5	6	7	8	9	10
✓	✗								
11	12	13	14	15	16	17	18	19	

The answer to this puzzle is in the **Answer Section**, at the back of the book.

Presentation tips (1) *Before the presentation*

1. Plan, prepare, practice (▸page 126, stages 1, 2, and 3).
2. Find out about your audience (Who are they? What do they expect from you?).
3. Dress suitably for the audience and the occasion.
4. Arrive early and check the equipment (▸page 126, stage 4).
5. Have a backup plan ready, in case there is a problem with the equipment.
6. Have your handouts ready and give them to the audience before you start (▸page 126, stage 4).
7. Breathe deeply. Collect your thoughts.
8. Smile (▸page 126, stage 4).

Presentation tips (2) *During the presentation*

1. Keep eye contact with the audience.
2. Don't rush. (Pause and take breaths.)
3. Speak clearly and project your voice (or use a microphone).
4. Use the 'signpost language' effectively (▸pages 123–125).
5. Have prompt notes or cards.
6. Refer to the visual aids, but don't read them. (The audience can read!)
7. Be aware of your body language, gestures, posture, and movement.
8. Smile.

No one can remember
more than three points.
(Philip Crosby)

Presentation tips (3) *Handling questions*

1. Welcome the question.
2. Listen carefully to the question. (Don't interrupt.)
3. Check that you have understood the question.
4. Take time to think before you answer.
5. Reply positively (brief and clear).
6. Accept criticism positively.
7. After the answer, check that the questioner is satisfied.
8. Smile.

Presentation tips (4) *After the presentation*

1. Ask yourself 'How did it go?'
2. Ask a friend who was there to give feedback.
3. Make a note of problems that you had. Think about how to overcome them.
4. Think about what you would change if you could do it again.
5. Ask yourself 'Did I enjoy it?' Then ask 'Why?' or 'Why not?'
6. Ask yourself 'Did I do my best in all four stages?'
7. Think about what you have learned. Think about how you have grown.
8. Smile. Don't punish yourself. You will do better next time.

Presentation checklist

Here is a group presentation checklist. Check the items as you move through the 4 stages of the presentation process.

		☐
☐ **Planning**	○ Ask questions about the topic.	☐
	○ Brainstorm ideas together.	☐
	○ Make notes of the points you want to cover.	☐
	○ Assign roles to group members.	☐
☐ **Preparing**	○ Collect data.	☐
	○ Arrange data into a logical sequence.	☐
	○ Make notes for the presentation.	☐
	○ Make audio/visual materials.	☐
☐ **Practicing**	○ Go through your part of the presentation by yourself.	☐
	○ Time yourself. See how long it takes.	☐
	○ Get a friend or family member to watch you and give advice.	☐
	○ Record your voice and listen to it.	☐
	○ Practice in front of a mirror and watch your body language.	☐
	○ Practice as many times as possible.	☐
	○ Remember your speech. (Don't read!)	☐
	○ Rehearse, rehearse, rehearse.	☐
☐ **Pre-presenting**	○ Check the presentation room.	☐
	○ Check the seating layout (audience).	☐
	○ Check the heating/air-conditioning.	☐
	○ Check the lighting and the sound system.	☐
☐ **Presenting**	○ Begin and end on time.	☐
	○ Give handouts to the audience before the start.	☐
	○ Use notes to help you remember.	☐
	○ Keep to the structure of the presentation (page 123).	☐
	○ Use signposting language (pages 123–125).	☐
	○ Check your body language, delivery, and appearance.	☐
☐ **Assessing**	○ Assess your performance using the self-assessment sheet on page 134.	☐
	○ Assess the other groups using the peer-assessment sheet on page 135.	☐

Presentation self-assessment

How was your presentation? Did you do your best in every stage? Did you perform your part well? Circle the (%) that matches your efforts.

Before the presentation

1. I helped choose a topic (page 122).

0%	25%	50%	75%	100%

2. I helped in the planning stage (page 127).

0%	25%	50%	75%	100%

3. I helped in the preparation stage (page 128).

0%	25%	50%	75%	100%

4. I practiced by myself (pages 126, 129).

0%	25%	50%	75%	100%

5. I used English with my group members in stages 1 to 3.

0%	25%	50%	75%	100%

6. I rehearsed the presentation with my group.

0%	25%	50%	75%	100%

7. I studied the presentation language on pages 123 to 125.

0%	25%	50%	75%	100%

8. I studied the presentation tips on pages 131 and 132.

0%	25%	50%	75%	100%

During the presentation

9. I followed the presentation structure (page 123).

0%	25%	50%	75%	100%

10. I remembered my speech.

0%	25%	50%	75%	100%

11. I spoke clearly, without hesitation, and without rushing.

0%	25%	50%	75%	100%

12. I was confident and cheerful.

0%	25%	50%	75%	100%

13. I made eye contact with the audience.

0%	25%	50%	75%	100%

14. I wore smart clothes.

0%	25%	50%	75%	100%

15. I controlled my body language, body posture and positioning.

0%	25%	50%	75%	100%

Presentation peer-assessment

How were the group presentations? Were they well prepared? Was the content interesting? Enter the numbers that match their efforts.

4 = Excellent ; 3 = Good; 2 = Not bad; 1 = Poor.

1. General Organization	Gp 1	Gp 2	Gp 3	Gp 4	Gp 5
□ Was the presentation well prepared?					
□ Was there a clear structure (beginning, middle, end)?					
□ Was the content relevant and interesting?					
□ Was the timing well managed?					
2. Delivery (Verbal Communication)	Gp 1	Gp 2	Gp 3	Gp 4	Gp 5
□ Did they speak clearly?					
□ Did they speak at the right speed?					
□ Did they use appropriate language?					
3. Body Language (Non-verbal Communication)	Gp 1	Gp 2	Gp 3	Gp 4	Gp 5
□ Were their body gestures natural?					
□ Did they maintain eye contact with the audience?					
□ Did they appear confident and positive?					
4. Audio-Visual Aids (mp3, handouts, board, flash cards)	Gp 1	Gp 2	Gp 3	Gp 4	Gp 5
□ Were the audio-visual aids clear and effective?					
□ Did the audio-visual aids support the group's message?					
□ Did the group use the equipment well?					
5. Overall Impression (including Q&A attitude)	Gp 1	Gp 2	Gp 3	Gp 4	Gp 5
□ Did they consider the audience?					
□ Did they dress suitably?					
□ Did they handle questions well?					
Total Score (maximum = 64)					

Group 1: comments and suggestions	
Group 2: comments and suggestions	
Group 3: comments and suggestions	
Group 4: comments and suggestions	
Group 5: comments and suggestions	

Freshman English 1: Review Corner

How was this course? Fill in this course-assessment sheet.

1. How was the course?	
2. How was the textbook?	
3. How was the teacher?	
4. How were the other students?	
5. How were my assignments?	
6. How was my groupwork?	
7. How were my self-assessments?	
8. How was my presentation (▸page 134)?	
9. How are my speaking skills now?	
10. How are my writing skills now?	
11. What can I do well now?	
12. What do I need to improve?	
13. What was the most impressive thing in this course?	
14. How can this course be improved?	

Cut out this page and give it to the teacher.

WELCOME TO THE WB

Word Bank

This resource will help you improve your English speaking and writing. Check it out regularly and use the words and phrases whenever you can.

Contents

Feelings and emotions

adorable
affectionate
afraid
alive
ambitious
angry
annoyed
anxious
ashamed
awkward
bad
beautiful
blue
bold
bored
brave
calm
capable
cautious
childish
clumsy
comfortable
compassionate
competitive
confident
confused
content
curious
daring
delighted
depressed
determined
disappointed
discouraged
doubtful
eager
embarrassed
emotional
energetic
enthusiastic
envious
excited
fantastic
fearless
foolish
fortunate
free
friendly
frightened
frustrated
glad
good
grateful
great
greedy
guilty
happy
hateful
helpless
homesick
honored
hopeful
horrible
humble
impatient
important
inspired
intelligent
interested
involved
jealous
jolly
joyful
lazy
lonely
lost
loved
loving
marvelous
miserable
naughty
negative
nervous
optimistic
overjoyed
overworked
passive
peaceful
pessimistic
pleased
powerful
proud
puzzled
quiet
regretful
relaxed
relieved
ridiculous
rude
sad
safe
satisfied
scared
selfish
sensitive
sentimental
serious
shy
sick
sleepy
smart
so-so
special
strong
stubborn
stupid
surprised
suspicious
sympathetic
tense
terrible
terrific
thankful
tired
uncomfortable
uneasy
unhappy
warm
wise
wonderful
worried

Positive qualities

active
affectionate
amusing
artistic
aware
capable
careful
caring
cheerful
clever
comical
competent
confident
considerate
cooperative
courageous
courteous
creative
dependable
devoted
earnest
easygoing
efficient
energetic
enthusiastic
forgiving
friendly
funny
generous
gentle
good-hearted
good-humored
good-natured
happy
hard-working
helpful
heroic
honest
honorable
humble
humorous
idealistic
imaginative
independent
intelligent
interesting
inventive
joyous
keen
kind
kind-hearted
lighthearted
lively
logical
lovable
loving
loyal
mature
merciful
natural
objective
open-minded
organized
original
outgoing
patient
playful
pleasant
polite
practical
rational
reasonable
reflective
reliable
resourceful
respectful
responsible
sensible
sensitive
sincere
skillful
sociable
sympathetic
tender
thorough
thoughtful
trustworthy
truthful
understanding
unique
unselfish
warm
warm-hearted
wise
witty

Location - prepositions

in	from	up	front	between	at the top of	to the left of
on	near	down	back	opposite	at the bottom of	to the right of
of	next	left	across	middle	in the center of	far from
to	far	right	behind	center	in the middle of	across from

Parts of the body

toe	ankle	knee	abdomen	shoulder	wrist	finger	neck
foot	calf	thigh	chest	arm	hand	thumb	head
heel	leg	stomach	torso	elbow			

Parts of the face

chin	teeth	moustache	nose	eyelash	eyebrow	forehead	scalp
lips	dimples	jaw	nostrils	eyelid	ears	temple	hair
mouth	beard	cheek	eyes				

Hair

bald	braids	curly	Mohican	receding	thinning
black	brown	dyed	perm	red hair	wavy
bleached	brunette	fuzzy	pigtails	straight	white
blonde	bun	gray	ponytail		

Compund adjectives - people

rosy-cheeked	blue-eyed	easy-going	broad-shouldered
slim-hipped	average-looking	good-natured	hot-headed
curly-haired	absent-minded	quick-witted	pig-headed
suntanned	broad-minded	flat-footed	quick-tempered
thin-lipped	open-minded	left-handed	self-centered
warm-hearted	cold-hearted	long-legged	

Self-assessment words

Personal qualities (Unit 2)

ability
caution
confidence
courage
creativity
diligence
effort
fairness
friendship
generosity

honesty
hope
intelligence
justice
kindness
logical
maturity
motivation
organization
patience

persistence
respect
responsibility
self-discipline
sensitivity
sincerity
surprise
trust
wonder

anger
anxiety
enthusiasm
fear
happiness
joy
passion
pity
pride
sadness

excellent
good
not so good
poor
better
positive
improving
increase
decrease
success

Learning skills (Unit 4)

high/low
more/less
change
effort
believe
encourage
improve
regular

careful
honest
diligent
hard-working
motivated
responsible
sincere
thoughtful

achievement
cooperation
collaboration
diligence
enthusiasm
passion
sharing
trust

strategies
analyzing needs
setting goals
time-management
reflecting
assessing
evaluating

Social awareness (Unit 10)

bigger/smaller
better/worse
improve
increase
decrease
change
more/less
global/local
international

transportation
traffic jams
parking
commuting
inflation
recession
litter
pollution
recycling

art
dance
drama
music
literature
opera
painting
poetry
philosophy

charities
museums
galleries
donating
sponsoring
volunteering
cooperation
contribution
participation

current affairs
education
GDP
government
health
human rights
immigration
law, police
politics

Marking code and paragraph checklist

Code	Problem	Example
C	Capitalization	C C C C C my name is gary. i come from the isle of man. My Gary. I Isle Man
P	Punctuation	P P P P P I like music. movies: and hiking? How, about you! music, movies, and hiking. How about you?
Gr1	Apostrophes Personal pronouns	Gr1 Gr1 Gr1 Thats not mine dog. Im certain about that. That's my I'm
Gr2	Singular/plural Count/non-count	Gr2 Gr2 Gr2 Gr2 Nobody have eaten many meats or fruits. has much meat fruit
Sp	Spelling	sp sp sp sp The trainn doesn't arive at the staytion untill 5 pm. train arrive station until
Pr	Prepositions	Pr Pr Pr Put the square in top about the circle and next the cube. on of next to
Art	Articles	Art Art Art ~~The~~ Hallasan is ^ highest mountain in ~~the~~ South Korea. the
S/v	Subject/verb agreement	S/v A large percentage of the population are watching the World Cup. is
WO	Word order	WO My sport favorite is fencing.

✓	Paragraph Checklist
☐	Title
☐	Topic sentence
☐	Unity (only one idea)
☐	Cohesion 1 (smooth flow of ideas)
☐	Cohesion 2 (pronouns, articles, transitions)
☐	Continuity (each sentence leads into the next)
☐	Concluding sentence

Sample editing

E-mail (Unit 1, page 9) first draft

To: J.Brown@eflteach.com

Subject: Hi teacher! :)

Attach a file | Receipt On Read : ☐ | Receipt On Delivery : ☐

Cc | Bcc | Signature | Addresses | Save Draft | Send | Check Spelling

Too informal

Hey, teacher,

Capitals = shouting

C how's it going? C i'm Kim Ji-seok. C call me Dave.

I'M SO HAPPY TO BE IN YOUR CLASS. ^^ Emoticons - informal

C how long ru in Korea? C where did you come from?

C how old ru? C what do you think Korea?

Wrong topic. This e-mail is a self-introduction.

C i'm born in Seoul. My family is 4 people. C father works in the bank and mother works supermrket. my sister studies high school.

C i like music. movies, and hiking. C my sport favorite is basketball. C i will be businessman. Haha. Too informal

btw, I hope this homework is ok. i did my best. ㅠㅠ Emoticons - informal

cu next class ... bfn ☺ Texting language (btw, cu, bfn) too informal

E-mail (Unit 1, page 9) after rewriting (draft 2)

To: J.Brown@eflteach.com

Subject: My introduction (Kim Ji-seok)

Attach a file | Receipt On Read : ☐ | Receipt On Delivery : ☐

Cc | Bcc | Signature | Addresses | Save Draft | Send | Check Spelling

Dear teacher,

Please let me introduce myself. My name is Kim Ji-seok. My English name is Dave. I was born in Seoul and there are four people in my family. My father works in a bank and my mother works in a supermarket. My sister studies in high school. I like music, movies, and hiking. My favorite sport is basketball. I hope to be a businessman.

One paragraph, instead of lots of single sentences.

Best wishes

Dave (Kim Ji-seok)
Class: Composition 101

MC's Q & A cards

(Unit 10 ▸page 114)

Water: 5 points	Water: 10 points	Water: 15 points	Water: 20 points
The largest hydroelectric power station in the world is in which country? China, Brazil, USA, Russia (Answer: China)	The largest tidal power station in the world is in which country? South Africa, Northern France, Norway, Mexico (A: Northern France)	Tidal turbines produce energy when the tide is moving in or out. How many hours does this happen each day? 5 hours, 10 hours, 15 hours, 20 hours (Answer: 10 hours)	When a lake was made for hydroelectricity in New Zealand, which city had to be moved? Cheviot, Canvastown, Cromwell, Christchurch (Answer: Cromwell)
Solar: 5 points	**Solar: 10 points**	**Solar: 15 points**	**Solar: 20 points**
The first solar cell was made by Charles Fritts in which decade? 1780s, 1840s, 1880s, 1920s (Answer: 1880s)	Albert Einstein was awarded a Nobel Prize in 1931 for his work on solar and photovoltaic experimentation. True or false? (Answer: True)	Enough sunlight reaches the earth's surface each hour to provide the whole world with power for how long? One week, One month, One year, One decade (Answer: One year)	Which British astronomer used a solar collector box to cook food while he was in Africa in 1830? Newton, Herschel, Lassell, Airy (Answer: Herschel)
Bio: 5 points	**Bio: 10 points**	**Bio: 15 points**	**Bio: 20 points**
Bio-fuels are a major source of power in which country? Australia, Canada, Brazil, Russia (Answer: Brazil)	What is biomass? Organic matter, Radioactive waste, Diet food, Non-vegetable waste (A: Organic matter)	What are some examples of biomass? Wood, Skeletons, Crops, All of these (Answer: All of these)	Biomass provides the USA with what % of its energy needs? 1%, 3%, 5%, 13% (Answer: 3%)
Geo: 5 points	**Geo: 10 points**	**Geo: 15 points**	**Geo: 20 points**
The first examples of geothermal power in the world were volcanoes and geysers. True or false? (Answer: True)	Iceland stands on a volcanic system, which provides most homes with geothermal energy. True or false? (Answer: True)	The first geothermal heating was created in 1948 by a professor in which university? Harvard, Oklahoma, Hawaii, Ohio (Answer: Ohio)	The Geysers in northern California produce enough power for how many homes? 1 million, 2 million, 3 million, 5 million (Answer: 2 million)
Wind: 5 points	**Wind: 10 points**	**Wind: 15 points**	**Wind: 20 points**
In which city did Charles Brush build the first automatic wind turbine in 1888? Cleveland, Amsterdam, Los Angeles, Paris (Answer: Cleveland)	Where is the largest wind turbine in the world? Holland, Hawaii, China, Saudi Arabia (Answer: Hawaii)	One wind turbine can meet the electrical needs of how many homes? 100, 200, 300, 500 (Answer: 300)	In 2008, which continent led the world in the development of offshore wind power? Asia, America, Africa, Europe (Answer: Europe)

Discussion words and phrases, Transition words

The words and phrases in this section can be used in the speaking and writing activities in this book.
The informal expressions (in blue) are not used in formal writing.

Adding a point | 내용 추가할 때

First,	Besides,	What's more,	Equally important,	Oh I almost forgot …
Second,	Moreover,	Furthermore,	In the same way,	And another thing
Next,	In addition,	As well as …	Not only … but also	Just a small point
Also,	Likewise,	On top of that,	Not only that but …	That reminds me …
Again,	Similarly,	For example,	Plus the fact that …	
	Otherwise,	For instance,	Not to mention that …	

Advantages and disadvantages | 장단점 표현할 때

On the one hand,
On the other hand,
One advantage is that …
One disadvantage is that …
The positive side of it is that …
The negative aspect of it is that …

The problem is …
One drawback is that …
Another thing is that …
I'm afraid to say that …
The main advantage is that …
The main disadvantage is that …

Advice | 조언할 때

Have you thought about … ?
I advise you to …
I think you ought to …
I think you should …
I think you'd better …
If I were in your place, I'd …
If I were in your position, I'd ....

If I were in your shoes, I'd …
If I were you, I'd …
It is advisable to …
One way would be to …
Perhaps you could …
The best thing for you to do is …

What about …ing?
Why don't you … ?
Why not … ?
You'd better …
You could always …
Your best bet is to …

Advice after the event | 어떤 일이 발생한 후 조언할 때

What you should have done was….
You shouldn't have …
You should have …
I wouldn't have done that.

Why didn't you……?
If I had been you, I would have….
You really should have asked me.

Agreement and disagreement | 찬성과 반대 표현할 때

True. Yes.
I agree. I disagree.
I don't agree.
That's right.
That's true.
That's very true.
Yes, of course.
I agree with you that ...
I know what you mean.
You are absolutely right.

Agreed.
Me too! So do I.
OK. Right.
I couldn't agree more.
I agree with you there.
You are absolutely right.
That's what I thought.
I'll go along with that.
That's what I thought.

I can't agree.
Absolutely not
Of course not.
That's not possible.
You can't be serious.
I think you are mistaken.
We'll have to agree to differ.
Yes, but don't you think …?
Yes, but on the other hand …

Approval and disapproval | 승인/찬성과 반대의견 표현할 때

Excellent.
Very good.
Well done.
I approve of …
I disapprove of …
I don't enjoy …

I love it.
It's great!
Marvelous.
Wonderful!
Fantastic!
I'll give it 10.
I think it's fantastic.

It's my cup of tea.
It's out of this world.
It's not for me.
It's not my cup of tea.
It doesn't turn me on.
It doesn't do anything for me.
I'm afraid I disapprove of ...

Argument and counter argument | 주장과 반론을 제기할 때

The first thing to point out is …
Let us look at the facts.
One argument in support of...
The second reason for...
It is a well-known fact that...
It is often said that...
On the other hand …

Anyway,
OK, but …
Yes, but …
Even so,
Possibly, but …
That's true, but …
But don't forget …

But what about …
Even if that is so,
Look at it this way.
That may be so, but …
Yes, but don't forget …
You have a point, but …
That's probably true, but …

Asking for clarification | 설명 요청

Can you explain … ?
Can you say that again?
Do you mean to say … ?
Does this mean …?
How come …?
What did you say?
What do you mean by …?
Why do you say that?

Asking for opinions | 의견 물을 때

How about you?
What do you think?
What would you say?
Do you have an opinion?
What do you think of ...?
Do you agree with the others?
What's your opinion of/about ...?
Would you like to tell us your opinion?

Asking for repetition | 한번 더 말해 달라고 요청할 때

What did you say?
What was that again?
One more time, please.
Could you repeat that?
I'm sorry, I didn't hear you.
Could you say that again, please?
Would you mind repeating that?

Breaking in | 상대방 말 중단할 때

Excuse me. Sorry, but …
Can I come in here?
Can I add something?
Can I say something here?
I'd like to comment on that.
Excuse me for interrupting, but …
I don't want to interrupt, but …
May I interrupt for a moment?

Cause and effect | 원인과 결과 표현할 때

So,	Due to …	Therefore,	Otherwise,	For this reason,
Thus,	Since …	Wherefore	Thereupon	For these reasons,
Hence,	So that …	Accordingly,	Consequently,	For this purpose,
Then …	Because …	As a result,	Subsequently,	With the result that …

Certainty and uncertainty | 확신과 불확신 표현할 때

Certainly. Absolutely.	I'm convinced that …	I don't see how …
Of course.	I'm (am) certain that ...	I doubt whether …
No doubt.	I am sure that ...	Yes, but don't forget …
Without a doubt.	Yes, but …	I'm pretty sure that…
There is no doubt that ...	I'm not sure.	Yes, but the problem is …
The problem is …	Possibly, but …	What I'm worried about is …

Changing the subject | 화제 전환

Talking of …
By the way,
That reminds me …
Oh, before I forget, …
I'm sorry to change the subject, but …
It's funny you should say that, but …

Checking comprehension | 이해 체크

OK?	Do you follow?
OK so far?	Do you understand?
Do you see?	Does it make sense?
Are you with me?	Shall I say it again?
Is that clear?	Are you still with me?
Have you got it?	

Clarifying | 설명/해명/부연할 때

Let me explain.	I said … What I said was …
Let me put it this way.	I mean … I mean to say …
Let me put it another way.	What I meant was …
To put it more clearly,	What I'm saying is …
For example,	What I'm trying to say is ...

Comparison and contrast | 비교와 대조 표현할 때

As (adj) as …	Larger than …	Or … But …	In contrast,
As though …	Smaller than …	Yet … Still,	Rather than …
Likewise,	More (adj) than …	In fact,	Even when …
Similar to …,	More than …	Rather,	Even though …
Similarly,	Greater than …	Unlike …,	Nevertheless,
Better than …	Less than …	Instead,	On the contrary,
Worse than …	At the same time,	Whereas …	On the one hand,
Bigger than …	By comparison,	However,	On the other hand,

Comprehension and incomprehension | 이해 여부 표현할 때

Yes. I see.	OK. Right. I get it.
I understand.	Pardon?
I'm with you.	I don't get it.
Now I follow you.	You've lost me.
I see what you mean.	Sorry, you've lost me.
Now I understand.	Sorry, I don't follow you.
I don't understand.	Sorry, I didn't catch the last part.
I'm not with you.	I didn't understand a word you said.

Concession | 상대의 말에도 일리가 있고 옳다고 인정할 때

Of course.	All right.
You have a point there.	OK.
That's a good point.	If you say so.
I take your point.	Yes, that's true.
While that may be true,	You've got a point.
I can't argue with that.	That's true, but …

Deduction and reasoning | 연역에 의한 결론 및 추론

If…, then …	…, so it must be …	We can conclude that …
Therefore, …	This indicates that …	These arguments show that …
This means that …	This proves that …	These arguments suggest that …
It follows that …	This shows that …	This points to the conclusion that …

Direction | 방향을 표현할 때

here	nearly	across from	to the left	above	in the distance
there	opposite	far from	to the right	below	You can't miss it.
beyond	next to	over there	straight ahead	under	

Disappointment | 실망/유감 표현

Oh, no!
Oh, dear!
What a pity!
That's a pity.
What a shame!
It's a shame!
That's so sad.
How disappointing!
I feel (really) let down.
I feel really disappointed.
I don't know what to say.

Displeasure | 불쾌/불만 표현

I don't like it.
It's horrible/terrible!
I can't stand it.
I don't like to think of it.
It makes me sad/unhappy.
I can't tell you how sad/angry I was.

Emphasis | 강조할 때

Again,
Also,
Truly,
Really,
Surely,
Chiefly,
Besides,
Certainly,
In fact,
In truth,
Indeed,
Above all,
Of course,
Especially,
In addition,
Particularly,
Furthermore,

Expressing surprise | 놀람을 표시할 때

Are you sure?
That is amazing!
I can't believe it.
I am surprised.
I'm shocked.
That's extraordinary.
I'm surprised to hear that.
Oh? What?
Oh, really?
My goodness!
Good Heavens!
Are you joking?
You're pulling my leg.
That's one for the books.

Generalizing | 일반화시켜 표현할 때

Usually,
As a rule,
Generally,
In general,
Normally,
Ordinarily,
By and large,
On the whole,
In most cases,
For the most part,
In my experience,
Generally speaking,
More often than not,

Getting started | 시작할 때

Let's begin.
Shall I start?
Shall we begin?
How can we begin?
Let's get started.
Let's get the ball rolling.
Who would like to start?
Would someone like to kick things off?
Does anyone have something to say?

Giving an opinion | 자신의 의사/견해를 표현할 때

I think …
In my view,
As I see it, ...
My view is ...
To my mind,
I think (that) …
I suppose …
I suspect that …
In my opinion,
I believe that …
Well, personally,
I personally think …
It's my opinion that …
From my point of view,
Not everyone will agree with me, but …

Giving reasons | 방향을 표현할 때

First of all, …	For this reason, …	The main reason is …	The other reason is …
Secondly, …	Besides that,	The main thing is …	Another reason is …
That's why …	Because of that, …	On the one hand, …	And on top of that,
Because …	The reason why …	On the other hand, …	And finally,

Illustrating | 예시할 때

In this case,
For example,
As an example,
For instance,
For one thing,
For another thing,
As an illustration,

Making a point | 주장을 강조할 때

The point is …
My point is …
What I mean is …
What I want to say is …
We must remember that …
We have to remember that ...
We should not forget that ...

Pleasure | 즐거움/기쁨/만족 표현할 때

It's very pleasing.
It makes me feel good.
I am really delighted.
I cannot tell you how happy I am.
It gives me great pleasure.

Wonderful!
Fantastic!
I feel great.
How marvelous!
I'm really pleased.
I'm over the moon.

Predicting | 예측/예견

If …,
If I ever …
When …
Whenever …
As soon as …
By the time …
Unless …

Preference | 선호도 표현할 때

I prefer to …
I like to …
I love … ing
I would like to …
I really like to …
I would prefer to …
My preference is …

What do you prefer?
What do you like most?
I like apples more than bananas.
I prefer apples to bananas.
My favorite is ….
I'd rather have a cup of coffee.

Requesting | 요청할 때

Can I ask a question?
May I ask something?
Do you know … ?
I'd like to know …
I'm interested in …
Could you tell me .. ?
Do you mind if I ask a question?

Returning to the topic | 화제로 되돌아올 때

Anyway, …
In any case, …
As I was saying, …
Getting back to the topic, …
Where was I?
What was I saying?
To get back to what I was saying, …

Sequencing | 순서대로 나열하거나 시간 순서 표현할 때

Next,	For now,	At first,	In conclusion,	Since then,
Then,	In time,	First of all,	To begin with,	The next step is …
Soon,	In turn,	After that,	In the first place,	In the meantime,
Earlier,	Later on,	Meanwhile,	At the same time,	Simultaneously,
Later,	Finally,	Afterwards,	For the time being,	With this in mind,

Stating the issue | 문제를 제시하거나 진술할 때

The trouble is …	The point is …	The thing is …	The real question is …
The problem is …	The real problem is …	Don't forget that …	

Suggesting | 제안할 때

Let's ... Why not … ?
I suggest ...
I've an idea.
How about … ?
Why don't you … ?
You can always ...
Do you feel like ...?
Have you ever thought of ...?

Surprising facts | 놀라운 사실 전할 때

Surprisingly,
Oddly enough,
Strangely enough,
Do you realize that …?
Believe it or not,
The surprising thing is …
It may sound strange but …
You may not believe it but …

Summarizing | 요약하거나 결론을 도출할 때

Briefly,	In short,	In any case,	On the whole,	In the long run,
In brief,	Finally,	In any event,	In summary,	All things considered,
After all,	By and large,	To sum up,	To summarize,	As I have shown,
All in all,	On balance,	In conclusion,	Therefore,	

Synthesis | 논리적으로 종합할 때

Actually,	To be honest,	We can safely say that ...
Frankly,	It's fair to say that …	The truth of the matter is …
On balance,	In the final analysis, ...	The fact of the matter is that…
On reflection,	To tell you the truth,	

Wants, needs and wishes | 필요/요구/희망사항 표현할 때

I want to …	I prefer ...	I fancy ...	I wouldn't say no to …
I need to …	I would like to …	If only …	I wouldn't mind ...
I wish …	I am quite anxious to ...	I feel like ...	Wouldn't it be nice if …?

Glossary of key words

A

abbreviation 생략, 약어
ability 능력
Aborigine 오스트레일리아 원주민
above all 특히, 우선 첫째로
above ~보다 위에
abroad 외국으로(에), 해외로(에)
absent-minded 방심상태, 멍한
absolutely 절대로, 정말그렇다.
abundant 풍족한
accelerate 가속하다, 촉진하다
accept 받아들이다, 수락하다
access 접근
accident 사고, 재난, 우연
according to ~에 의하면
accordingly 따라서, ~에 맞게
accounts (업무)회계장부
accuracy 정확(성)
accurate 정확한
achieve 이루다, 성취(달성)하다
achievement 업적, 공로
acquire 얻다, 취득하다
across (~을) 가로질러, 건너편, (퍼즐) 가로열쇠
act 행동하다, 시늉, 법령
action 행동, 활동, 작용, 조처
active 적극적인
activity 활동
actualize 현실화하다
actually 사실은, 실제로는
acute 날카로운, 심각한
adapt 적응하다(시키다)
add 더하다, 덧셈하다
additional 부가적인, 추가의
address 주소, 연설(=speech)
adjective (품사) 형용사
admire 사모하다, 찬탄하다
adorable 사랑스러운, 귀여운
adult 성인
advance 진보, 발전, 진급
advantage 장점, 이득, 우세
adventure story 모험담
adverb (품사) 부사
advice 조언, 충고
Aesop's Fables 이솝우화
affair 일, 업무, 사건
affect 영향을 미치다
affectionate 애정 깊은, 다정한
affective 감정(정서)적인
afraid 두려워하여, 걱정하여
Africa 아프리카
afternoon 오후
afterwards 후에, 나중에
again 다시
age 나이, 성년(come of age)
agree with 동의하다
aid 돕다, 원조하다, 원조물
aim 목적, 목표(삼다), 겨누다
air 공기
air conditioning 냉방
airplane 비행기
air pollution 공기(대기)오염
alert 방심 않는, 기민한
alive 살아 있는, 민감한
all over the world 전 세계에
allow 허락하다, 허가하다
almost 거의
alone 혼자, 다만 ~만, ~뿐
along with 같이, 동시에
also 또한, 역시
alternative energy 대체 에너지
alternative power sources 대체 동력자원
alternative 대안(적인)
always 늘, 항상, 언제나
amazing 놀랄 정도의, 굉장한
ambitious 대망을 품은, 거창한
America 아메리카, 미주
Amsterdam 암스테르담
amusing 재미있는, 유쾌한
analysis 분석, 분석표
analyze 분석하다
ancestors 조상, 선조
ancient 옛날의, 고대의
angry 성난, 화난
animal 동물, 짐승
animation, anime 만화영화
ankle 발목
annoy 귀찮게 굴다, 괴롭히다
anonymous 익명의, 작자불명의
another 또 하나(의)
answer 대답(하다), 해답, 해결
anti-war 전쟁 반대의, 반전
anxiety 불안, 걱정, 근심
anxious 불안한, 초조한
anything 무엇이든, 아무것도
anyway 여하튼, 어떻게 해서든
apology 사과, 사죄
apostrophe (부호) 아포스트로피
appear 나타나다, ~인 듯 하다
appearance 외모, 출현
apple 사과
application 적용, 지원(서)
apply 적용하다
approach 방법, 접근(법)
appropriately 적절하게
approve 승인(허가, 찬성)하다
April 4월
Arabia 아라비아
area 지역,영역, 구역
argument 주장, 논의, 요지
arm 팔
around 주위(에), 근처
arrange 배열하다, 준비하다
arrive 도착하다
arrow 화살
art 예술, 미술, 기술
article (문법) 관사
artificial 인조의, 부자연스런
artificial intelligence 인공 지능
artistic 예술적인
as well as ~뿐만 아니라
Ash Wednesday 사순절의 첫날
ashamed 부끄러운, 수줍어하여
Asia 아시아
asleep 잠들어
assess 평가하다
assessment 평가, 진단
assign 할당하다, 배분하다
assignment 숙제, 과제(물)
asterisk 별표
astronomer 천문학자
at least 적어도
at once 즉시

athlete 운동 선수
attachment 붙임, (컴퓨터)첨부
attend 참석하다
attention 주의, 배려
attitude 태도, 자세, 몸가짐
attract 끌다, 유인하다
audience 청중, 관객
auditory 귀의, 청각의
August 8월
Australia 호주, 오스트레일리아
authentic 진정한, 인증된
automatic 자동의, 기계적인
A/V 시청각(의) (audio visual)
avalanche 눈사태
average 평균, 표준
average-looking 보통으로 생긴
Avignon 아비뇽 (남프랑스 도시)
avoid 피하다, ~하지 않다
awareness 의식, 자각, 인식
awkward 어색한
axe 도끼

B

baby 갓난아이
back 후면, 뒤로
backup (컴퓨터)백업, 예비의
bad 나쁜
balance 균형(을 맞추다)
bald 대머리의
ball 공, 무도회
balloon 풍선
ballpoint pen 볼펜
banana 바나나
bankrupt 파산한, 빚투성이인
bark 나무 껍질
base 기초를 두다
basic 기초적인, 근본의, 기본, 기초
basketball 농구
battery 배터리, 건전지
battle 전쟁, 전투, 투쟁
beach 해변, 바닷가
bean 콩, (콩 비슷한) 열매
bean paste 된장
beard 수염
beat 연달아 치다, 이기다
beautiful 아름다운, 예쁜
because ~한 이유로, ~때문에

become ~이 되다
beer 맥주
begin 시작하다, 착수하다
beginning 시작, 초기
behavior 행실, 행동
behind 뒤에
Belgium 벨기에
believe 믿다, 신용하다
below 밑에
benefit 이득, 이득, 혜택
Berlin 베를린
besides 게다가, 그 밖에
better 더 나은
between 사이에
beyond ~저쪽에, ~을 넘어서
bicycle 자전거(=bike)
BIFF 부산국제영화제 (Busan International Film Festival)
big 큰
billiard ball 당구공
billion 10억
biofuel 바이오연료, 생체연료
biography 전기문학, 일대기
biomass 바이오매스
birch 자작나무
birth 탄생, 출생, 태생
bite (동물이나 모기 등이) 물다
black 검은, 블랙의(커피)
blame 나무라다
bleached 표백한
bless 축복하다, 은총을 내리다
blind 눈먼, 장님의, 맹목적
block (길 등을) 막다, 방해하다
blog 블로그
blonde 블론드의, 금발의
blood 혈액
blouse 블라우스
blue 푸른, 기분이 우울한
blue-eyed 푸른색 눈을 가진
blueberry 블루베리
board game 보드 게임
boat 보트, 배
body (연설, 글의) 본론, 몸, 신체
body language 보디 랭귀지
boil 끓다
bold 대담한
bone 뼈, 골격
border 테두리, 가장자리
bored 지루한

born 타고난, 태어나다
bottom 아래쪽, 하부, 밑바닥
bowl (밥 등의) 한 그릇, 우묵한 접시
bowling 볼링
boy 소년, 아들
brackets 괄호
braids 땋은 머리
brain 두뇌
brainstorm 브레인스토밍하다
brainstorming 브레인스토밍 (각자 아이디어를 떠올려 모아보기)
branch (나무의) 가지, 지점, 출장소
brave 용감한, 화려한, 놀라운
Brazil 브라질
bread 빵
break 깨뜨리다, (잠깐의) 휴식
breakfast 아침식사
breakthrough 돌파구, 큰 발전
breathe 숨쉬다, 호흡하다
bridge 다리, 연결
briefly 간단히, 짧게
bright 빛나는, 똑똑한
Bristol 브리스톨(영국남서부) 도시
broad-minded 관대한
broad-shouldered 어깨가 넓은
broccoli 브로콜리
brother 동생
brother-in-law 처남, 매부, 자형
brown 갈색
brunette (머리색이) 거무스름한
Buddha 부처님
buffet 뷔페(식) 식당
bug 곤충
build 세우다, 조립하다
building 건축, 건물
bun 둥그런 빵 (햄버거 등에 씀)
burger 햄버거
burglar alarm 자동 도난 경보기
burn 불타다, 불태우다, 화상
burnout (스트레스로) 심신 소모
burst 파열하다
business 비즈니스, 업무, 일, 용건
busy 바쁜
butter 버터
butterfly 나비
by oneself 혼자

C

cabbage 양배추
cafeteria 카페테리아(셀프서비스 식당)
calcium 칼슘
California 캘리포니아
calligraphy 서예
calm 침착한, 진정시키다
calories 칼로리
camel 낙타
camera 카메라
campus (대학)캠퍼스
Canada 캐나다
cancel 취소하다, 중지하다
cancer 암
candle 양초
capable 유능한, 실력 있는
capital 수도, 자본
capitalization 대문자 사용
Cape Town 케이프 타운
car 차, 자동차
car crash 자동차 충돌사고
carbohydrates 탄수화물
carbon fuel 탄소 연료
career 직업, 경력
careful 조심성 있는, 신중한
caring 사려깊은, 인자한
carnival 카니발, 축제행사
carpet 양탄자, 카펫
carrot 당근
carry 운반하다, 휴대하다
carry on 계속하다
cartoon 만화, 만화영화
case 경우, 사건
castle 성, 성곽, 대저택
catch 붙들다, 잡다, 이해하다
cause 원인
cautious 주의 깊은, 신중한
Celsius 섭씨의(=centigrade)
celebrate 축하, 경축하다
cell 세포, (전기) 전지
cell phone 휴대전화
cement 시멘트, 결합하다
center 중심, 중심에 두다
century 1세기, 백년
CEO (chief executive officer) 최고 경영자
ceramics 도자기류
cereal 곡류, 아침식사용 곡물식
certainly 확실히, 반드시, 물론이오.
challenge 도전(하다)
challenging 해 볼 만한
championship 선수권 대회
chance 기회, 우연, 승산
change 변경하다, 바꾸다
character 인물, 성격
characteristic 특징, 특색
chart 도표, 차트
chat 이야기(하다), 잡담(하다)
check 점검하다
checklist 점검목록, 체크리스트
cheek 뺨
cheerful 기운찬, 즐거운
cheese 치즈
chemicals 화학 물질
chest 가슴
chew 씹다
chiefly 주로, 대개
childish 어른답지 못한, 유치한
children 아이들, 어린이, 자식
chin 턱
China 중국
chocolate 초콜릿
choose 고르다, 선택하다
chop 자르다
chopsticks 젓가락
Christian 기독교의, 기독교도
chronic 만성의
cinema 시네마, 영화(관)
circle 원, 동그라미를 치다
circulate 유포(순환)하다
citizen 시민
city 도시
civil war 내란, 내전
claim 요구(청구, 주장)하다
clan 씨족(=tribe)
clarify 해명하다, 정화하다
class 종류, 등급
classify 분류하다
classmate 급우, 클래스메이트
clean 청결한, 청소하다
clear 명백한, 깨끗한, 투명한
clearly 똑똑히, 분명하게
Cleveland 클리블랜드
clever 영리한, 눈치 빠른
climate 기후
climate change 기후변화
clipboard 필기받침대, 클립보드
clock 시계
clone 클론, 복제 생물/인간
close 가까운, 닫다, 마감하다
clothes 옷
cloud 구름
clumsy 서투른, 재치없는
coal 석탄
coast 연안, 해안
coated 겉에 바른, 방수가공한
coffee 커피
coherence 통일성, 일관성
cohesion 문장 간 결속성
cohesive 결속성(결합성) 있는
cold 추운, 찬, 차게 식은
cold-hearted 냉담한
collaborate 협력하다
collaboration 협력
collect 모으다, 수집하다
college (단과)대학
collocation 연어(=natural word combination), 자주 함께 쓰이는 단어결합 및 숙어
colon 구두점의 콜론
colony 식민지
color 색, 빛깔
column (표나 도표의) 열, 칸
coma 코마, 혼수상태
comb 빗
come 오다, 가다, 도착하다
comeback 회복, 컴백
comedy 코미디, 희극
comfortable 편안한, 아늑한, 마음 편한, 쾌적한, 만족을 주는
comic strip 연재 만화
comical 우스꽝스러운, 익살맞은
comma 구두점의 쉼표
comment 논평(하다), 말하다
committee 위원회
common 일반적인, 공통의
communicate 의사소통하다
communication 의사소통
community 공동(지역)사회
commute 통근(통학)하다
company 회사, 친구, 동행자
compare 비교하다
comparison 비교
compassionate 인정 많은
compete 경쟁하다, 다투다
competent 유능한

competition 경쟁
competitor 경쟁자, 라이벌
complain 불평하다
complete 완성하다, 완벽한
complex (심리적) 콤플렉스
comprehend 이해하다
comprehension 이해
computer 컴퓨터
computer crash 컴퓨터 시스템의 고장
concentrate 집중하다, 응집하다
concert 콘서트, 음악회
concise 간결한
conclude 결론짓다, 끝내다
conclusion 결론
condo 콘도, 공동주권
conduct (전기) 전도하다
confidence 자신감
confident 자신(감) 있는
confused 혼란한
congratulate 축하하다
conjunction (문법) 접속사
connect 연결하다
consequence 결과, 귀결
consequently 따라서, 결과로
conservation 보존, 유지
consider 고려하다, 배려하다
considerate 이해(배려)심 있는
consist of (~로) 구성되다
constant 끊임없이 계속하는
consumer awareness 소비자 의식
contact 연락처, 연락하다
contain 담고 있다, 포함하다
content 내용, 목차, 만족하여
contest 경쟁, 논쟁
context 컨텍스트, 문맥, 상황
continent 대륙
continue 계속하다, 지속하다
continuity 연속성, 지속
contrast 대조(하다), 현저한 차이(를 보이다)
control 지배(통제)하다, 관리
convenient 편리한
conversation 대화, 이야기
convert 전환하다, 바꾸다
convince 확신시키다
cook 요리하다, 요리사(=chef)
cool 멋진, (열을) 식히다
cooperation 협조
copy 베끼다, 모방하다, 복사하다
corn 옥수수
corner 모퉁이, 구석, 코너
correct 옳은, 정확한
cosmetics 화장품, 미용의
cosmos 우주
cotton 면, 솜, 탈지면
couch 긴 의자, 소파(=sofa)
count your blessings (불행한 때에) 좋은 일들을 회상하다
counter 반대의, 한쪽편의
country 국가, 나라
courageous 용기 있는, 용감한
course 과정, (대학)교과목, 강좌
court 법원, 법정
courteous 예의 바른
cover 덮개, 뚜껑, 덮다
craft 공예(품)
crayon 크레용, 색연필
crazy 제정신 아닌, ~에 열광한
create 창조하다, 만들다
creation 창조(물)
creative 창조적인, 독창적인
creative thinking 창의적 사고
credit card 신용 카드
critical 비판적인, 중대한
critical thinking 비판적 사고
criticism 비평, 비난
crop (수확한)농작물, 곡물
crowd 군중, 다수, 관중
cruise ship 유람선, 관광선
crust 빵 껍질, 딱딱한 표면
culture 문화
cup 컵
curator 관리자, 큐레이터
cure 치료하다, 고치다
curiosity 호기심
curly-haired 곱슬머리의
current affairs 시사문제(뉴스)
custom 관습
cut 베다, 절단하다, 끊다
cut out 잘라내다
cycle 순환, 순환기
cycling 사이클링, 자전거 타기

D

daily 매일의, 일상의, 일간신문
daily routines (매일 반복되는) 일과
dairy (우유, 치즈, 요구르트 등) 유제품(의), 낙농장
dance 춤, 무용, 춤추다
danger 위험
daring 대담한
dark 어두운
data 데이터, 자료
data collection 자료 수집
database 데이터베이스
day 낮, 하루
dead 죽은, 활기 없는, 폐기된
deal with 다루다, 처리하다
dealer 중개인, 상인, 업자
death 죽음, 종말
debating 토론, 논쟁
decade 10년간
decide 결정하다, 결심하다
decision-making 의사결정
Declaration of Independence 미국 독립 선언 (1776. 7. 4)
decrease 감소(하다)
deduction 추론
deed 행위, 행동
deep 깊은, 깊이(심도) 있는
defendant 피고, 피고인
deficiency 부족, 결핍
definite 한정된, 명확한
definition 정의, 의미
degree 정도, (온도 등의)도
delicious 맛있는, 상쾌한
delighted 기뻐하는
deliver 배달, 전달하다
delivery 전달, 의사전달 능력, 이야기투, 말투
demonstrative pronoun (문법) 지시대명사
deodorant 탈취제
depend 의존(의지)하다, ~에 달려 있다
dependable 믿을 수 있는
depressed 우울한, 낙담한
describe 묘사하다, 설명하다
description 설명, 묘사
desert 사막
design 디자인하다, 설계하다
desk 책상
destroy 파괴하다
destruction 파괴
detail 세부사항, 자세한 내용
detergent 합성 세제

determined 결의가 굳은, 단호한
develop 개발하다, 발전시키다
developed country 선진국
development 발달, 개발, 발전
device 기구, 장치, 고안품
devoted 헌신적인
diagram 도형, 도표
diary 일기, 일지
dice 주사위
die 죽다, 사멸하다, 활동을 멈추다
die out 사멸하다, 소멸하다
diet 식사, 영양섭취, 식이요법
differ (의견이나 모습 등이) 다르다
different 다른
difficult 곤란한, 어려운
digestion 소화, 소화 작용
diligence 부지런함, 성실함
dimples 보조개
dinner 저녁 식사
dinosaur 공룡
direction 방향, 설명, 약도
director (영화)감독, 연출
disadvantage 단점
disagree 의견이 다르다
disappear 사라지다
disappointment 실망
disapprove ~을 안 된다고 하다, 찬성하지 않다
discharge (전기)방전, 제대하다
discouraged 낙심한, 낙담한
discover 발견하다
discovery 발견
discuss 토론하다, 의논하다
disease 질병
dish 요리, 접시
distressed 고뇌에 지친, 어려운
diverse 다른 종류의, 다양한
diversity 다양성
divide 나누다, 분할하다
Diwali 디왈리 (인도의 축제)
doctor 의사, 박사
document 문서, 서류
dog 개
dominant 지배적인, 널리퍼진
dos and don'ts 지켜야 할 사항들
doubt 의심, 의심하다
doubtful 의심스러운, 못 미더운
down 아래로, (퍼즐)세로열쇠
downtown 시내
draft 초안, 초고
drain 물을 비우다, 물기를 없애다
drama 드라마, 연극, 희곡
draw 그리다, (선을) 긋다
drawback 약점, 장애
dream 희망, 꿈
dress 옷을 입다, 옷
dress up 옷을 차려 입다
drink 마시다, 마실 것
drive 운전하다, ~한 상태로 만들다
driving test 운전 면허 시험
drop 물방울, 떨어뜨리다, 버리다, 그만두다
drought 가뭄
drown 익사하다
dry 마른, 말리다
due to ~할 예정인, ~의 탓인
during ~동안
dust 먼지, 가루, 먼지를 털다
duty 의무, 임무, 관세
duty-free shop 면세점
DVD 디지탈 영상 디스켓(Digital Video Disc)
dyed 염색한, 물들인

E

e-mail 이메일(electronic mail)
each 각자의, 각각의
eager 열망하는, 열심인
ear 귀
early 일찍, 이른, 초기의
earn 벌다, 획득하다
earnest 진지한
Earth 지구
earthquake 지진
easily 쉽사리, 순조롭게
east 동쪽, 동양(the East)
Easter 부활절
easy-going 태평한, 안이한
eat 먹다
economics 경제학
edit 교정보다, 편집하다
Edinburgh 에딘버러 (스코틀랜드의 수도)
education 교육
educator 교육자, 교육가
effect 결과, 효과
effectively 효과적으로
efficient 능률적인
effort 노력
egg 달걀, 알
Egypt 이집트
elastic 탄력(성) 있는, 고무줄
elbow 팔꿈치
elderly 나이가 지긋한, 상당한 연배의
elect 뽑다, 선거하다, 선임하다
electricity 전기
elementary school 초등학교
e-mail address 이메일 주소
embarrassed 당황한, 난처한
emigrate (타국으로) 이주하다
emission 방사, 배기
emoticon 이모티콘
emotional management 감정 관리
emotions 감정, 감동(감격)
empty 빈, 공허한, 허탈한
encourage 격려하다, 권하다
encyclopedia 백과 사전
end 끝, 결말, 최후, 목적(=aim)
energetic 원기왕성한, 활동적인
energy 에너지, 활기, 원기
engineer 기술자, 공학자
English 영국(인)의, 영어의
enjoyable 즐거운, 재미있는
enlarge 크게 하다, 확장하다
enough 필요한 만큼, 충분히
entertainment 여흥, 오락, 연예
enthusiastic 열심인, 열성적인
envious ~을 부러워하는
environment 환경
episode 에피소드, 삽화적 사건, (TV, 라디오) 연속물의 1회분
equally 같게, 동등하게
equipment 장비, 설비, 비품
escape 탈출하다, 달아나다, 모면하다, 벗어나다
especially 특히
esteem 존중, 존경의 마음
ethics 윤리(관), 도덕(관), 도의
ethnic 소수 민족 일원, 민족 특유의
Europe 유럽
evaluation 평가
event 사건, 사고, 결과
eventually 결국(은), 드디어
every 모든
everyone 각자 모두, 누구든지

everything 모든 것
everywhere 어디에나
evidence 증거(물), 흔적, 증언
exam 시험
examine 검사하다, 조사하다
example 예, 견본(=sample)
excellence 탁월(성)
excellent 탁월한
excited 들뜬상태의, 흥분한
exclamation mark (구두점) 느낌표
Excuse me. 실례합니다.
exercise 운동, 훈련하다
exist 존재(실재)하다, ~에 있다
expand 확장하다, 팽창하다
expect 기대하다
expensive 비싼
experience 경험
experiment 실험(하다)
expert 전문가, 명인, 달인
explain 설명하다, 해명하다
explanation 설명, 해명
explode 폭발하다, 파열하다
explore 탐험하다, 탐구하다
exposure 노출(시간)
express 표현하다, 나타내다
expressive ~을 나타내는, 표정(표현)이 풍부한
external 외부의
extraordinary 비상한, 비범한
extravagant 낭비벽이 있는, 엄청난
extremely 매우, 극도로
eye 눈
eye contact 시선 마주침
eyebrow 눈썹
eyeglasses 안경
eyelash 속눈썹
eyelid 눈꺼풀

F

fable 우화, 꾸며낸 이야기
fabric 직물, 짜임새(=texture)
face 얼굴, 체면, 외관
fact 사실
factor 요소, 요인
factory 공장
Fahrenheit (온도)화씨
fail 실패하다
failure 실패, 쇠약, 낙오자
faith 신념, 믿음, 신앙심
false 잘못된, 허위의, 그릇된
fame 명성, 인기
familiar 익숙한
family 가족
famous 유명한
fancy 공상(하다), 좋아함
fantastic 굉장한, 기상천외의
far from ~에서 멀리
farewell 작별, 작별인사
farming 농업, 농장
fashion 패션, 유행
fast 빠른, 단식하다
fast food 즉석 식품, 패스트푸드
fat 지방
fatal 치명적인, 운명의
fate 운명
father 아버지, 선조, 창시자
fault 잘못, 과실
favorite 좋아하는, 즐기는
fax machine 팩스기
fear 두려움, 공포
fearless 두려움이 없는
feature 얼굴생김새, 특징, 특색
feed 먹이를 주다, 먹이다
feedback 의견, 반응, 피드백
feeling 감각, 느낌, 감정
feminism 페미니즘
fertilizer 비료
festival 축제
fever 열, 열광, 열중
fewer 보다 소수의
fiber 섬유, 섬유질 식품
field 분야, 영역, 현장, 들판
fight 싸우다, 논쟁하다
fill 채워 넣다
filling 속에 넣는 것
film 영화
film festival 영화제
film star 인기 영화배우
finally 마지막으로
financial 재정(상)의, 금융의
find out 발견하다, 알아내다
finger 손가락
fire 불, 난방기, 화재
first 첫(번)째의, 맨 처음, 최초
first name (성에 대하여) 이름(=given name)
fish 물고기, 낚시하다
fit (꼭)맞는, 몸 상태가 좋은
flash cards 플래시 카드
flat 평평한
flat-footed 편평족의, 평발의
flaxseed 아마씨(=linseed)
float 띄우다, 뜨다
flood 홍수, 범람하다
floor 마룻바닥, 바닥
flow 흐름
flower 꽃
fluency (말이) 유창함
fly 날다, 비행하다
focus 맞추다, 집중시키다
follow 따라가다
food 음식
food, clothing and shelter (인간생활의) 의식주
food intake 음식 섭취량
foolish 어리석은
foot 발, 밑부분, 최하부
football 축구
footprint 발자국
for example 예를 들면
forehead 이마
foreign 외국의
foreigner 외국인
forever 영원히
foreword 머리말, 서문
forget 잊다, 생각이 안 나다
forgiving 용서하는
form 양식, 형식, 서식
formal 정식의, 정중한(영어)
format 형식
fortunate 운이 좋은
fortune 행운, 재산
fortune-teller 점쟁이
forward 앞으로, 전방으로
fossil fuel (석탄 등의) 화석연료
fountain 분수
France 프랑스
frankly 솔직하게
free 자유로운, ~이 없는
fresh 새로운, 신선한
freshman (대학)신입생, 새내기
Friday 금요일
fried rice 볶음밥
friend 친구
friendship 우정

fries 감자 튀김
frightened 깜짝 놀란, 겁이 난
frog 개구리
from ~에서, ~부터
front 앞으로, 전방
fruit 과일
frustrated 실망한, 욕구불만의, 좌절된
frying pan 프라이팬
fuel 연료
full 가득한, 가득 담긴, 풍부한, 배부른
full name 성명 (성+이름)
fun 즐거움, 재미있는 경험
function 기능, 기능을 다하다
funny 우스운
further 후속의, 더 나아간
furthermore 더욱이, 게다가
future 미래(의)
fuzzy 솜털같은, (생각 등이) 희미한, 분명치 않은, 술취한

G

gadget 기구, 소도구, 기계
gain 얻다
gallery 화랑, 미술관
gambit (대화의) 실마리, 작전
game 놀이, 게임
gas 기체, 가스
gender 성, 성별
general 전반(종합)적인, 일반의
general readers 일반 독자들
generalize 일반화(보편화)하다
generate 발생시키다, 낳다
generation 세대
generation gap 세대차이
generous 관대한
genetic 유전자의
genetically modified 유전자 변형의
genre 장르
gentle 온화한, 점잖은
geography 지리, 지형
geologist 지질학자
geothermal energy 지열 에너지
Germany 독일
gesture 제스처, 동작
geyser 간헐(온)천, 분출하다
girl 소녀, 여자아이, 딸
give 주다, 공급하다
give up 포기하다, 그만두다
glacier 빙하
glad 기뻐서, 기쁜
glass 유리, 잔
glasses 안경
global issue 전 세계적 문제
global village 지구촌
global warming 지구온난화
globalism 세계적 규모의 정책(사고방식), 세계주의
globalization 국제화, 세계화
glossary 어휘, 용어풀이
glue 풀, 접착제
goal 목표
goal-setting 목표설정
gods 신, 신과 같은 것
goldfish 금붕어
golf ball 골프 공
good 좋은
Good afternoon. 안녕하십니까.
Good heavens! 맙소사!
Good morning. 안녕하십니까.
good-hearted 마음씨 고운
good-humored 쾌활한, 상냥한
good-natured 마음씨 착한, 온순한, 사람이 좋은
government 정치, 정부, 정권
grade 성적, 점수를 매기다
gradually 점차적으로
graduate 졸업하다
grains 곡물, 곡류, 알갱이
grand 웅대한, 화려한
graph 그래프
grateful (호의, 은혜에) 감사하는
graveyard 묘지
gravity 중력
gray 회색
great 큰, 굉장한, 위대한
grandfather 조부, 할아버지
grandmother 조모, 할머니
Greece 그리스
greedy 탐욕스러운
green 녹색의, 환경 친화적인
green movement 환경보호 운동
greenhouse effect 온실 효과
greenhouse gas 온실 효과 가스
greeting 인사, 인사말
groundbreaking 혁신적인
group 그룹, 조, 모임
grow 성장하다, 자라다
guide 안내(서), 지침(서)
guilty 유죄의, 죄책감이 드는
guitar (악기) 기타
gum 고무, 껌, 잇몸
gym 체육관(=gymnasium)

H

habit 버릇, 습관
habitat 환경, 거주환경, 서식지
hair 머리카락, 털
half 절반
hand 손, 건네주다
handle 다루다, 처리하다
handout 유인물, 인쇄물
hang 걸다
Hanukkah (유대교 기념일) 하누카
happen (어떤 일이) 일어나다
happiness 행복, 즐거움
happy 행복한, 즐거운, 기쁜
Harbin (중국) 하얼빈
hard 단단한, 굳은, 곤란한, 어려운, (성격이) 무정한
hard-and-fast 엄격한
hard-working 근면한, 열심인
harmony 조화, 화합, 화음
harvest 수확, 수확물, 수확하다
hat 모자
hate 싫어하다, 하고 싶지 않다
hateful 미운, 싫은, 증오에 찬
Hawaii 하와이
head 머리, 두뇌, 선두, 꼭대기
headline 신문기사 표제, 방송 뉴스 주요 제목
health 건강, 위생, 보건
healthy 건강한, 건강상 좋은
heart 심장, 마음, 열의, 중심
heat 열, 열기, 가열하다, 데우다
heating 가열, 난방(장치)
heavy traffic 극심한 교통량
hectare 헥타르 (1만 m^2)
heel 뒤꿈치, (신발)뒤축, 말미
heir 남자 상속인, 후계자
help 돕다, 도움
helpful 도움이 되는, 유용한
helpless 의지할 곳 없는, 무력한

hence 그러므로, 지금부터
herb 허브, 식용향료식물
herbal medicine 한약
hero 영웅, 위인, 남자주인공
heroic 영웅적인, 과감한
hesitation 주저, 망설임
hide 숨기다
hierarchy 계급, 계층, 위계질서
high 높은, 고위의, 고급의
high school 고등학교
highlight 가장 중요한 부분, 주요 장면, 하이라이트
highlighter (pen) 형광펜
hiking 도보여행, 하이킹
hint 힌트, 넌지시알림, 낌새
history 역사
hit 때리다, 치다, 명중하다, (생각이) ~에게 떠오르다
hobby 취미
hold 손에 쥐다, 잡다
holiday 휴일, 휴가, 축(제)일
Holland 네덜란드(the Netherlands)
hollow 텅빈, 우묵한
home 가정, 자택, 고향, 본국, 본고장, 발상지
home-cooked 가정요리의, 집에서 요리해서 만든
homesick 향수병에 걸린
homestead 집과 대지, 택지
homework 숙제, 사전준비
honest 정직한, 진실한
honesty 정직(함)
honorable 존경할 만한, 고귀한
honored 명예로운
hope 희망, 바라다
Hopi (북미 인디언) 호피족
horrible 끔찍한, 무서운, 잔혹한
horse 말
hospital 병원
hot-headed 성미 급한
hour 시간, 시각, ~때
however 그러나, 하지만
huge 거대한, 막대한
human 사람의, 인간적인, 인간에게 흔히 있는
human right 인권
humble 겸손한, 겸허한, 초라한
hunger 배고픔, 기근, 갈망
hunt 사냥하다
hydroelectric 수력 전기의
hydrogen (화학) 수소
hydropower 수력 전기
hyphen (구두점) 하이픈

I

ice age 빙하기
icecap 만년설
Iceland 아이슬란드
ice-rink 스케이트장
icon 아이콘, 상, 형상
idea 생각, 의견
idealistic 이상주의적인, 공상적(비현실적)인
identify 확인하다, 신원을 밝히다, ~와 동일시하다
identity 정체성
ignore 무시하다
illness 병
illustrate 설명하다
imagination 상상력
imaginative 상상의
immediately 즉시, 바로
immigrant (타국에서의) 이주자, 이민
immune system 면역 시스템
impatient 조급한, 참을 수 없는, ~을 못 견디는
important 중요한, 중대한
improve 향상되다, 나아지다
in addition 게다가, 그 위에
in spite of ~에도 불구하고
incident 사건, 생긴 일
include 포함하다
income (정기적인) 수입, 소득
increase 증가, 증가하다
indeed 참으로, 실로, 과연
indefinite 불명확한, 무기한의
indent (문단 첫행을) 들여쓰다
independent 독립한, 자력의
India 인도
Indian (미국)아메리칸 인디언
indicate 가리키다, 지적하다
indigenous 토착의 (native), 원주민의
individual 개인, 개별적인
Indonesia 인도네시아
Industrial Revolution 산업 혁명
inequality 불균형, 차이
inference 추론, 함축
inferior (~보다) 못한, 하위의, 더 낮은
informal (말이) 일상 회화체의, 구어체의, 격식 차리지 않은
information 정보, 지식, 자료
informative 유익한
ingredient (요리의) 재료, 성분
inner 안의, 내부
innocent 결백한, 순진한
insect 곤충
inspire 격려하다, 영감을 주다
inspired 영감을 받은, 영감에 의한
instead 그 대신(에), 그보다도
instructor 강사
intake 섭취량
integrated 통합된, 융합된
intellectual 지적인, 지력을 요하는, 지식인
intelligence 지능, 지성, 사고력, 인텔리전스(정보요원)
intelligent 지적인, 지성을 갖춘, 영리한
interaction 상호작용, 대화
interactive 대화식의, 서로 영향을 주는, 상호작용하는
interesting 재미있는, 흥미로운
interface 접점, 공통영역
internal 내부의, 내면적인
Internet 인터넷
international 국제적인, 만국의
interpretation 해석, 설명, 통역
interrupt (도중에) 중단시키다, 가로막다, 저지하다
interview 인터뷰, 면접
intonation 억양, 어조
introduce 소개하다
introduction 서론, 소개
intuitive 직관적인, 직관력 있는
invention 발명(품), 지어낸 것
inventive 발명의(재능이 있는), 창의력이 풍부한
investigate 조사(연구)하다
investment 투자
invite 초대하다, ~을 청하다
involve 포함하다, 관련시키다, 수반하다
Iraq 이라크
Ireland 아일랜드
island, isle 섬
issue 문제(점), 논쟁(점), 발행하다,

(출판)발행부수
It's up to you. (결정은) 당신에게 달렸다.
Italy 이탈리아
item 항목, 품목, 조항, 물건

J

jacket 자켓
Jamaica 자메이카
Japan 일본
jaw 턱
jazz 재즈
jealousy 질투, 시기심
jeans 청바지
jeep 지프(자동차)
jet engine 제트 엔진
job 일, 직업
job application 취업지원서
join (함께)참여하다, 결합하다
joke 농담(하다)
jolly 유쾌한, 재미있는, 대단히
journalist 언론인
joyful, joyous 즐거운
judge 판사, 심사원
judgment 판단, 심판
July 7월
jump in ~에 뛰어들다
junior (대학) 3학년생, 나이가 ~보다 어린, 후배학생
junk food 정크 푸드, 인스턴트(즉석) 식품
just 바로, 바로 지금, 간신히, 다만, 좀, 정당한, 정의로운
justice 정의, 정당

K

kale (야채) 케일
keen 매우 관심 있는
keep 지키다, 지속하다
kick the bucket 죽다
killer 살인자
kind 친절한, 종류, 유형
kind-hearted (성격이) 친절한
kindness 친절, 친절한 행동
king 왕, 최고의 권위자
King Arthur 아서왕(의 전설)
kite 연
knee 무릎
know 알다, 숙지하다, 이해하다
knowledge 지식, 인식, 이해
koala bear 코알라(곰)

L

laboratory 실험실, 연구소
lack 부족하다, ~이 없다
lady 숙녀, 여성, 귀부인
lake 호수
land 토지, 착륙(상륙)하다
land-fills 쓰레기 매립지
landslide 산사태
language 언어, 말
lantern 초롱, 등, 랜턴
large 넓은, 큰
last 마지막의, 계속(지속)되다
late 늦은, 늦게
later 나중에, 후에
latest 최근의
Latin 라틴어, 라틴사람
laugh 웃다
law 법, 규칙
lawn 잔디
layer 층
layout 레이아웃, 기본틀, 구조
lazy 게으른, 태만한
leadership 리더십, 지도력
leaf 잎
learn 배우다, 공부하다
learner 학습자, 학생
learner-centered 학생 중심의
learning 배움, 학습
learning style 학습 스타일
leave 떠나다, (자리를)뜨다
lecture 강의, 강연
left 왼쪽(에)
left-handed 왼손잡이의
leg 다리
legend 전설, 구전하는 이야기, 전설적 인물
length 길이
Lent (기독교) 사순절
less ~보다 더 적은
lesson 수업, 강의
letter 편지, 글자
lettuce (야채) 상추, 양상추
level 수준, 단계
lexis 어휘
library 도서관, 서재
life 삶, 인생, 생명
lifelong 일생동안, 일생의
lifetime 일생, 생존기간
lift 올리다, 걷히다, 승강기
light 불, 밝은, 가벼운, (색깔이) 연한, 불을 지피다
light bulb (백열) 전구
light-emitting diode (LED) 발광 다이오드
lighthearted 쾌활한, 유쾌한
lightly 가볍게
like 좋아하다, ~와 같은
likely ~할 법한, ~할 듯한
likes and dislikes 좋아하는 것과 싫어하는 것
likewise 마찬가지, 또한
limit 제한(하다), 한계
link 연결(되다)
lining (옷의) 안감, 내층
lip 입술
lipstick 립스틱
liquid 액체(의)
list 표, 목록, 수록하다
listen 듣다, 경청하다
literacy 읽기 능력
literature 문학
litter 쓰레기(=trash, garbage)
lively 명랑한, 생기있는
liver (신체기관) 간
local 특정 지역의, 부분적인
location 위치, 위치의 선정
logical 논리적인
lonely 외로운, 고독한
long-legged 다리가 긴
look 보다, 모습
look after 돌보다, 간호하다
Los Angeles 로스앤젤레스
lose 잃다, (경기에) 지다, (몸무게를) 줄이다
lotion 로션, 외용 물약
lots of 많은, 상당한 수(량)의
loud 큰 소리로
lovable 사랑스러운
loved 사랑한, 소중한
lover 연인, 애인

low 낮은, (가격이) 저렴한
lower case letters 소문자
loyal 충성스러운
lucky 운이 좋은, 행운을 가져오는
lunar calendar 음력
lunch 점심 식사
lung (신체기관) 폐
luxury 사치, 사치품

M

machine 기계
magazine 잡지
magic 마법(의), 기막힌, 매력
magician 마법사, 마술사
magistrate 행정장관, 치안판사
maiden 처녀(의), 처음의
main 주요한, (제일)중요한, 주된, 주요 부분을 이루는
main idea 요점, 요지
maintain 유지하다, 관리하다
major (대학의) 전공 과목, 주요한, 대부분의, (군대)소령
make 만들다, 제작하다, ~이 되다, ~하게 하다
man-made 인조의, 인공의
manage 처리(관리)하다
management 관리
mankind 인류, 인간
manufacture 제작하다, 만들다
many 다수의, 많은
map 지도
Mardi Gras (축제) 마디그라
Marrakesh (모로코) 마라케시
March 3월
mark 점수, 채점하다
marketing (경제) 마케팅
marking code 교정(첨삭) 부호
marriage 결혼, 결혼생활
marry 결혼하다, 결합시키다
marvelous 놀랄 만한, 훌륭한
mask 가면, 탈, 마스크
massage 안마, 마사지
match 맞추다, 짝짓다, ~에 맞는 것을 찾아내다, 대항시키다
material 자료, 재료
matter 물질, 문제, 중요하다
mature 성숙한, 익은, 만기된
maximum 최대(한도), 극대의
Maya (중앙아메리카) 마야 족
MC 사회자, 사회를 보다
meal 식사
meaning 의미, 뜻
meaningful 의미심장한, 뜻 있는
meanwhile 그러는 동안
meat 고기, 육류
mechanics 기계적인 부분
medicine 의학, 약
medicinal 약용의, 약효 있는
meditate 명상하다, 숙고하다
meet 만나다, 충족시키다
Melbourne (호주) 멜버른
melt 녹다, 녹이다
melting pot (인종, 문화의) 도가니
member 단체의 한 사람
memorize 암기하다
memory 기억, 기억력
mental 정신의, 정신병의
mention 말하다, 언급하다
menu 식단표, 메뉴
merciful 자비로운, 인정 많은
message 전할 내용, 메시지
metal 금속
meteorology 기상학
methane 메탄
methanol 메탄올
method 방법, 방식, 순서, ~법
Mexico 멕시코
micro- 마이크로, 지극히 작은, 초소형, 초미니,
middle 중앙, 가운데, 중심
middle school 중학교
mile 마일
milk 우유
million 백만, 수백만
mind 마음, 지성, 주의하다
mind-map 마인드맵 (생각지도)
miner 광부, 광산 업자
mineral 광물, 미네랄
minority 소수 민족, 소수(임)
minute (시간의) 분, 잠시, 순간
mirror 거울, 반사경, 귀감, 비추다, 반영시키다
miserable 불쌍한, 비참한, 초라한, (날씨가) 구질구질한
mismatch 잘못 짝짓기
missing (있어야 할 곳에) 없는, 행방불명의, 실종된, 결석한
Mississippi (미국) 미시시피
mistaken 잘못된, 틀린, 잘못 생각하고 있는, 오해하고 있는
mix 섞다, 혼합하다
mixture 혼합물
mobile phone 휴대폰
model 모형, 모범, 본보기
modern 현대(식)의, 현대적인
Mohican 모히칸족
money 돈, 화폐, 금전
monkey 원숭이
monitor 감시(조정)하다, 검토하다, 추적하다
Montreal (캐나다) 몬트리올
moon 달, 달빛, (행성의) 위성
morality tale 도덕적 교훈을 담은 우화나 이야기
morals 교훈, 도덕, 몸가짐
more 더 많은, 보다 많이
moreover 그 위에, 또한
Morocco 모로코
mortally 치명적으로, 심하게
mostly 대개는, 대부분은, 주로
motivate ~에게 동기를 주다
motivation (행동의) 동기부여, 열의, 욕구, ~하고 싶은 기분
motorcar 자동차, 승용차
motto 모토, 표어, 좌우명
mountain 산, 산 같이 큰(높은)
mourn 슬퍼하다, 애도하다
moustache 콧수염
mouth 입, ~어귀, 말투, 어조
move 움직이다, 이동하다, 이사하다, 감동시키다
move on 계속 전진(진행)하다
movie 영화(=film)
movie genre 영화장르
mud 진흙, 머드
multilingualism 다언어 사용
multiple 여러, 다수의
multiple intelligences 다중지능
multiply 늘리다, 배가하다, (수학) 곱셈하다(by)
multivitamin 종합비타민제
mumble 중얼(웅얼)거리다
Munich (독일) 뮌헨
muscle 근육
museum 박물관

music 음악
music genre 음악 장르
musical instrument 악기
musician 음악가, 작곡가
My goodness! 저런, 어렵쇼
mysterious 신비한, 불가사의한, 설명할 수 없는, 미궁의
myth 신화, 신에 관한 이야기
mythical 신화의, 신화적인, 가공의, 공상의

N

nail 손톱, 발톱, 못, 못을 박다
nail polish 매니큐어
name 이름, 이름을 짓다
nano- 나노, 10억분의 1
narration 서술, 이야기(하기)
narrow 폭이 좁은, 마음(도량)이 좁은, 편협한, 좁은 의미의
national 국가의, 전국적인
national holiday 국경일
national park 국립공원
nationality 국적
natural 자연의, 자연스러운
natural resources 천연자원
naughty 장난스러운, 말을 듣지 않는, 도리에 어긋난
near 가까이, 가까운
nearly 거의, 대략, 간신히
nebula (천문학) 성운
necessary 필요한, 필수의
neck 목, (그릇의) 잘록한 부분
need 필요, 부족, ~을 필요로 하다, ~할 필요가 있다
needs 필요(요구) 사항
negative 부정적인
negotiate 협상, 교섭하다
neighbor 이웃, 이웃에 있는
nervous 긴장되는, 불안한, 소심
Netherlands 네덜란드
neuroscience 신경과학
never 절대 ~하지 않다, 절대로
nevertheless 그럼에도 불구하고, 그렇지만
new 새로운, 새로 나온, 신식의
newborn 갓난, 새생의
New Orleans (미국) 뉴올리언즈
news program 뉴스프로
newspaper 신문
next 다음의, 그 다음의
next to ~의 옆에, ~다음으로
night 밤
nightclub 나이트클럽
Nobel Prize 노벨상
nobleman 귀족
nobody 아무도 ~않다, 보잘것없는 (하찮은) 사람
none 조금도 (아무도) ~않다
nonprofit 비영리의
nonverbal 비언어적인
normal 정상의, 보통의, 통상
northern 북부(지방)의
Norway 노르웨이
nose 코
nostril 콧구멍
note 메모(하다), 적어두다, 주목하다, (화폐)지폐
note pad (사무용품) 공책
Notting Hill (런던) 노팅힐
noun (품사) 명사
novel 소설
now 지금, 현재, 이제부터
nuclear 핵의, 원자력의
nuclear family 핵가족
nuclear reaction 핵반응
nut 너트, 견과류
nutrients 영양소, 음식
nutrition 영양, 영양공급(섭취)
nutshell 견과껍질, 요약하다 (in a nutshell 아주 간결하게, 짧게)
nylon 나일론

O

obesity 비만
obey 복종하다, 말을 잘 듣다
object (문법) 목적어, 물건, 목적
objective 객관적인, 편견 없는
occasion 경우, 때, 축전, 행사
occur (사건이) 일어나다, (머리에) 떠오르다
October 10월
offer 제공하다, ~을 권하다
office 사무실, 임무, 직무
official 공식, 직무상의
offshore 앞바다의
often 자주, 흔히
Ohio (미국) 오하이오
oil 기름, 유화 물감
oil-rig 석유 굴착 장치
Oklahoma (미국) 오클라호마
old 오래 된, 나이 많은
old-fashioned 구식의, 고풍의
on the whole 대체로
on time 정각에, 제시간에
onion 양파
online 온라인, 온라인으로
open 열다, 시작하다
open-minded 편견이 없는
opinion 의견, 견해
opportunity 기회
opposite 맞은편의, 정반대의
optics 광학
optimistic 낙천주의의, 낙관적
oral test 구두 시험
orange 오렌지
order 순서, 명령, 차례
ordinary 평범한, 보통의
organ (생물의) 신체기관
organic 유기농으로 재배한
organic food 유기농 자연식품
organization 조직, 체제
organize 조직하다, 만들다
original 최초의, 본래의, 독창적
others 다른(딴) 사람들, 딴 것
otherwise 그렇지 않으면
outcome 결과, 성과
outer 밖의, 외부(외면)의
outer space 대기권 밖 공간
outgoing (성격이) 외향적인, 사교적(개방적)인, 은퇴하는
outline 윤곽, 개요
output 산출, 출력
outside 외부
overall 전체로, 전반적인
overcome 이겨내다, 극복하다
overgeneralize 지나치게 보편화시키다
overjoyed 매우 기뻐하는
oversleep 너무 오래 자다
overworked 과로한
owner 주인, 소유자
oxygen (화학) 산소

P

page 페이지, 책장
pail 양동이, 들통, 버킷
paint 칠하다, 그리다, 페인트
painting 그림, 페인팅
pair 한 쌍, 한 벌
pairwork 짝지어 하는 활동
palm 손바닥
panel 토론자단(심사원단), 패널, (캔버스 대용의) 화판
paper 종이, 서류, 신문, 논문
paper clip 클립, 종이 물리개
parachute 낙하산
paragraph 문단, (문장의) 단락
paraphrase 말 바꿔쓰기, 부연, 말을 바꿔서 설명하다
Pardon? (무슨 말씀인지) 다시 한 번 말씀해 주십시오.
parent 부모, 조상
parenthesis 괄호
parenthood 친자관계
Paris 파리
park 공원, 주차하다
parking 주차
participation 참여, 참가
particle 분자, 입자
particularly 특별히, 특히
partner 상대, 협동자, 배우자
pass (exam) 합격하다
pass on 넘겨주다, 전하다
passage 인용부분, 통행, 경과
passenger 승객
passion 열정, 매우 좋아하는 것
passive 수동적인, 소극적인
past 과거, 지나간, 과거의
past tense (문법) 과거 시제
pasta 파스타
pastime 기분전환, 소일거리
path 길, 좁은 길, 통로, 행로
patient 인내심이 강한, 끈기 있는
pause 잠시 멈춤, 중지, 중단
pay 지불(지급)하다, 봉급, 임금
pea 완두콩
peace 평화
peel ~의 껍질을 벗기다
peer-assessment 동료평가
penicillin 페니실린
people 사람들
pepper 고추, 후추
percent 퍼센트(%)
perfect 완전(완벽)한, 더할 나위 없는, 결점이 없는, 이상적인
perform 수행하다, 연기하다
perfume 향수
perhaps 아마, 어쩌면, 형편에 따라서는, 혹시 ~일지도 몰라
period 기간, (구두점) 마침표
perm (머리를) 파마하다
persecution (종교적인) 박해
Persia 페르시아
person 사람, 인간, 인물
personal 개인의, 개인적인
personality 개성, 성격, 인물
pessimistic 비관적인
pesticide 농약, 살충제
pet 애완 동물
petroleum 석유
philosopher 철학자
photovoltaic (물리) 광기전성의
phrase 문구, 구절, 표현
physical 신체의, 물리적인
physiological 생리학적인
picture 그림, 상상하다
piece 조각
pig-headed (부정적) 고집센
pigtails 땋아 늘인 머리
pillow 베개, 밑에서 받치다
pilot 파일럿, 조종사
pirate 해적
place 장소, 놓아두다
plan 계획, 계획하다
plastic 플라스틱, 성형의
play 놀다, 연주하다, 놀이, 연극, 각본, 희곡(drama)
playful 쾌활한, 농담 좋아하는
pleasant 즐거운, 기분 좋은, 호감이 가는, (날씨가) 좋은
pleased 기뻐하는, 만족한
plot 플롯, (극, 소설) 줄거리
plug in (전기) 플러그를 끼우다
plural (문법) 복수, 두 개 이상
pocket 호주머니, 포켓
poem, poetry (문학) 시
point 한 곳, 점, 요점
point of view 관점, 견해
point out 지시하다, 지적하다
polar 극지의, 남극(북극)의
pole (천문학) 극, 극지
police 경찰
polite 공손한, 예의바른
politely 공손하게
political 정치적인, 정치의
pollution 공해, 오염
polymer 중합체, 폴리머
ponytail 포니테일(뒤에서 묶어 아래로 드리운 머리)
pool 물웅덩이, (인공) 작은 못
poor 가난한, 가엾은, 서투른, 부족한, 건강치 못한
pop culture 대중문화
popular 대중의, 인기 있는
popular (=pop) music 대중음악
population 인구
portfolio 과제를 넣는 보관집
position 위치, 지위, 입장, 견해
positive 확신하는, 긍정적인
possession 소유(물), 소지, 재산
possible 가능한
post-reading (책을) 읽은 후의
postcard 우편 엽서
poster 포스터
posture (앉은, 서 있을때) 자세
pot 냄비 (a tea pot 찻주전자)
poultry (식용의) 새(닭)고기
pour (액체를) 따르다, 쏟다
poverty 가난, 빈곤, 결핍
power 힘, 전원, 동력, 능력
power plant 동력장치, 발전소
power station 발전소
powerful 강력한, 유력한, 설득력 있는
practical 실제의, 실용적인
practice 연습하다
pray 기원하다, 기도하다
predict 예언하다, 예보하다
prefer ~을 좋아하다, 선호하다
pregnancy 임신
preparation 준비
prepare 준비하다
present 출석한, 지금의, 현재의
presentation 발표
preserve 보존하다, 보호하다
president 대통령, 총장, 사장
pressure 압력, 누르기
previous 앞의, 이전의
printing press 인쇄기계
prior to 앞, ~보다 앞에

probably 아마, 필시, 대개는
problem-solving 문제해결
proceed 나아가다, 속행하다
process 과정, 진전, 프로세스
process writing 여러 단계를 거친 글쓰기 접근법, 쓰기과정
processed food 가공음식
produce 생산하다, 제조하다
producer 생산자, 제작자, 감독
product 결과(물), 소산, 성과
professional 전문적인, 직업적
professor 대학교수
profile 인물 소개, 프로필
profit 이윤
progress 발전, 진보하다
project 프로젝트, (음성을) 청중에게 분명하게 전하다
project-based 프로젝트 위주의
promote 촉진시키다, 증진
prompt 신속한, 촉구(유발)하다
pronoun (문법) 대명사
pronunciation 발음
proof 증거, 입증물
propane (화학) 프로판
propose 제안하다, 청혼하다
pros and cons 찬반, 장단점
protect 보호하다
protein 단백질
proud 자랑하는, 자랑스러운
proverb 속담
provide 제공하다
public speaking 남들 앞에서 말하기
public transport 대중교통
publish 출판하다, 발표하다
pulp 과육, 펄프
pump 펌프, ~을 밀어넣다
punctuation 구두점, 구두법
punish 벌하다, 응징하다
purple 보라색
purpose 목적
pursuit of happiness 행복 추구
puzzle 퍼즐(게임)
puzzled 당혹한, 어리둥절한
pyramid 피라미드, 피라미드형 조직

Q

quality 품질, 자질, 질 좋은
quality of life 생활 수준, 삶의 질
queen 여왕
question 문제, 질문하다
question and answer (Q & A) 질의 응답
question mark (구두점) 물음표
quick-tempered 성미가 급한
quick-witted 재치 있는
quickly 빨리
quiet 조용한, 고요한, 침착한
quite 아주, 매우, 상당히
quiz show 퀴즈 게임쇼
quotation 인용구, 인용문
quotation mark 인용 부호

R

race 인종, 경주
racism 인종(민족) 차별주의, 인종적 편견
radiation 방열, 발광
radio 라디오
radioactive 방사성의, 방사능의
radish (채소) 무
raise 올리다, 세우다
Ramadan (이슬람) 라마단 기간
random 무작위의, 임의의, 순서없이 되는 대로 하는
range 지식 범위
rank 등급, 평가하다
rapid 빠른, 신속한
rarely 드물게, 거의
rate 비율, 시세, 요금, 속도
rather 오히려, 꽤
rational 합리적인, 이성적인
read 읽다, 해석하다
ready 준비된
real 진짜의, 현실의
reality 진실, 사실, 현실, 실재
realize 깨닫다, 실현하다
really 참으로, 정말(이지)
rearrange 재배열하다
reason 이유, 이성
reasonable 분별 있는, 적당한, 무리 없는, 비싸지 않는
reasoning 추론, 추리력
recede 물러나다, 멀어지다
receive 받다, 받아들이다
recent 최근의
recipe (요리의) 조리법, 레시피
recognize 알아보다, 인정하다
record 기록, 기록하다
recover 되찾다, 회복하다
recreational 휴양의, 오락의
recycling 재활용
red 빨간, 붉은
red bean 팥
red hair 붉은색 머리
red meat 붉은 고기 (쇠고기 등)
red tape 관료적 형식(절차)에 얽매인
reduce 줄이다
refer 언급하다, 지시하다
reference 참조, 언급, 관련
reflect 반영하다, 반성하다
reflection 숙고, 재고, 반성
reflective 숙고하는, 반사적인
refresh 새롭게 하다
refrigerator 냉장고
refuse 거절하다, 거부하다
regarding ~에 관해서
regardless (of) ~에 관계없이
regretful 후회하는
regularly 규칙적으로
rehearsal 연습, 리허설
rehearse 미리 연습하다
relate 관련하다, 관련짓다
relationship 관계, 연관성
relative 친척, 상대적인
relax 마음 편히 갖다, 쉬다
relevant 관련된
reliable 의지할 수 있는, 믿을 만한
relieved (고통, 부담을) 경감한
religion 종교
remember 기억하다
remind 생각나게 하다
remove 옮기다
renew 새롭게 하다, 갱신하다
renewable energy 재생가능 연료
repeat 되풀이하다, 반복하다
reply 대답, 대답하다
reservation (북미 인디언을 위한 정부의) 지정 거류지
reservoir 저수지
resource 자원, 수단, 기지
resourceful 자원이 풍부한
respect 존경, 존중하다
respectful 공손한, 정중한

response 대답, 응답, 반응
responsibility 책임, 책임감
responsible 책임 있는, 신뢰할 수 있는
result 결과
resume 이력서(=CV)
retire 퇴직하다, 물러나다
return 되돌아가다, 돌려주다
review 복습, 재검토, 논평
revise 교정(수정)하다
revive 소생하다, 부활시키다
revolution 혁명, 회전, 순환
reward 보상, 보답, 사례금
rice 쌀, 밥
rich 부유한, 풍부한
riddle 수수께끼
ridiculous 어리석은, 우스운
right 옳은, 올바른, 오른쪽의
Rio de Janeiro 리오데 자네이로
river 강
road 길, 통로
road sign 도로 표지
robot 로봇, 자동 장치, 기계적으로 일하는 사람
role 배우의 배역, 역할
role play 역할극
roll 두루마리, 롤
roller 굴림대
Rome 로마 (이탈리아의 수도)
room 방, 장소, 공간
rope 밧줄, 끈, 밧줄로 묶다
rosy-cheeked 장밋빛 뺨
rotate 회전하다, 교대하다
round table 원탁
routine 일상의, 판에 박힌
royal 왕가의, 왕립의, 고귀한
rubber band 고무 밴드
rude 무례한, 교양이 없는
rule 규칙
run out (물이) 새다
rush 돌진하다, 급하게 행동하다, 덤비다
Russia 러시아

S

sacrifice 희생하다
sad 슬픈, 슬픈 듯한
safe 안전한
saint (종교) 성인
salad 샐러드
salmon 연어
salt 소금
same 같은, 동일한
sample 샘플, 견본
sandals 샌들 신발
sandwich 샌드위치
Sapporo (일본) 삿포로
satellite 위성
satisfy 만족시키다
sauce 소스
Saudi Arabia 사우디 아라비아
sauna 사우나(탕), 증기욕(탕)
save 구하다, 모으다, 저장하다
say 말하다
scared 겁먹은, 무서워하는
scarf 스카프
scene 장면, 광경, 현장
school 학교, 학파
science 과학, ~학
science fiction (SF) 공상과학
scientific 과학적인, 정확한
scientist 과학자
scope 범위, 영역
score 득점, 점수
screen 스크린, 화면
seafood 해산물
search 찾다, 살피다
seaside 해안의, 해변의
season 시즌, 철, 계절
seastead 해상 택지
seating 좌석, 좌석배치
second 둘째, 제2의, 또 하나의
secret 비밀의, 비밀, 신비스러운
section 구분, 절단, 자른 면
secular 현세(세속)의, 비종교적
secure 안전한, 안전하게 하다
security 안전, 보안, 담보
see 보다, 만나다, 이해하다
seed 씨앗
seem ~처럼 보이다
seize the moment (*Carpe Diem*) 현세를 즐기라
select 선택하다, 고르다
self-assessment 자기평가, 자가진단
self-centered 자기 중심의, 이기주의적인
self-esteem 자부(심), 자긍심
self-reliance 자기 신뢰, 자립
selfish 이기적인
sell 팔다
semester (대학의) 한 학기
semicolon (구두점) 세미콜론
semiconductor 반도체
Senate 상원
send 보내다, 부치다
senior (대학) 4학년, 상급생, 연장자, 연상의
sensible 분별 있는, 현명한
sensitive 민감한, 감수성 강한
sensitivity 감성, 민감도
sentence 문장, 선고하다
sentimental 감상적인
September 9월
sequence 순서, 차례, 결과
series 시리즈, 연속물(프로)
serious 진지한, 심각한
servant 하인
serving 음식을 차림, 음식시중
sesame 참깨
session 개회중임, 세션
sexism 성차별주의
shampoo 머리 감기, 샴푸
shamrock 토끼풀, 클로버
share 몫, 분배하다, 공유하다
sharing 함께 쓰는, 공유하는
sheet 시트, (종이) 한 장
shelter 피난장소, 숙소, 집
shirt 와이셔츠, 셔츠
shock 충격, 충격을 주다
shoes 구두
shoot 쏘다, 공을 차(던져) 넣다, 촬영하다
short 짧은, 작은, 불충분한
shortage 부족, 결핍
shoulder 어깨
shoulder-length 어깨까지 내려오는 길이
show 보이다, 안내하다, 나타나다
shower 샤워
Shrove Tuesday 성회 화요일
shy 소심한, 수줍어하는
sick 병에 걸린, 메스꺼운
side 측면, 옆구리, 가장자리
signal 신호, 징후, 신호하다
signature 서명
significant 중대한, 의미 심장한

signpost 이정표, 명확한 길잡이
silk 비단, 견직물, 실크
silly 어리석은, 바보 같은
silver 은, 은제품, 실버
similar 유사한, 비슷한, 닮은
simple 단순한, 간소한, 순박한
simultaneous 동시의
since ~이후, ~이므로
sincere 성실한, 진실한
sing 노래하다
sister 여동생
site 위치, 장소, 용지, 유적
skeleton 골격, 해골, 뼈대, 윤곽
skiing 스키 타기
skill 기술, 숙련, 노련, 능숙함
skillful 능숙한, 교묘한, 숙련된
skin 피부
skirt 스커트, 치마
slave 노예
sleep 잠, 잠자다, 활동 정지
sleepy 졸리는, 잠자는 듯한
slice 얇은 조각, 자르다, 썰다
slide 미끄러지다, (눈)사태
slim-hipped 호리호리한 엉덩이
small 작은, 얼마 안 되는, 적은
smart 컴퓨터화한, 고성능의, 말쑥한, 스마트한, 맵시 있는
smile 웃다, 미소짓다
smooth 매끄러운, 부드러운
snack 간식, 스넥
so 그래서, 그러므로
so far 지금까지
so-so 그럭저럭, 그저 그런
soap opera 연속 라디오/TV 멜로 드라마
soccer 축구
sociable 사교적인, 사귀기 쉬운
social qualities 사회성
social skill 사회적 (대인)능력
society 사회, 사교, 협회, 단체
soda water 소다수, 탄산수
soft 부드러운, 소프트
soft lenses 소프트 콘텍트렌즈
solar 태양광선 이용한, 태양의
solution (문제의) 해결, 해법
solve 풀다, 해결하다
something 무언가, 어떤 것, 대단한 사람(물건, 일)
son 아들
sonata (음악) 소나타, 연가
soon 곧, 일찍, 빨리
sophomore (대학) 2학년생
sort 종류, 분류하다
soul 영혼, 정신
source 원천, 출처
south 남쪽
South Africa 남아프리카 공화국
South Pole 남극
soy (=soy sauce) 간장
spaceship 우주선
Spain 스페인
sparingly 드물게
spawn (개구리 등의) 알
speak 말하다, 이야기하다
special 특별한, 개인용의
species (생물) 종
speech 말, 말하기, 연설
speech bubble (만화책 등의) 대사를 적거나 설명하는 공간
speed bump 과속 방지턱
speed of speaking 말하는 속도
spelling 철자, 철자법, 스펠링
spice 양념, ~한 맛
spinach 시금치
spiritual 정신의, 정신적인
spongy 작은 구멍이 많은
sport 운동, 즐거움, 장난
spread 펴다, 덮다
spring 봄, 샘물, 탄력
square brackets 꺽쇠괄호
squash 호박
squeeze 압착하다, 짜내다
staff 직원, 지팡이
stage 무대, 단계
stand 서다, 일어서다
star 스타, 인기배우, 인기인
start 출발하다, 시작하다
starve 굶주리다, 배고프다
statement 진술, 문장, 성명서
station 정거장, 역, 위치, 부서
status 상태, 지위, (법률) 신분
stay 머무르다, ~인 채로 있다
steel 강철
step 단계, 걸음, 스텝
stick 막대기, 지팡이
still 아직도, 그럼에도, 더욱
stimulate 자극하다, 고무하다
stir 휘젓다, 움직이다
stir-fry (요리) 재빨리 볶다, 그렇게 요리한 음식
stomach 위장, 복부, 식욕
stone 돌, 돌멩이, 바위
stop 멈추다, 그만두다
storage 저장, 보관, 창고
store 비축하다, 저장하다
story 이야기, (건물의) 층
storyline 줄거리(=plot)
storyteller (단편)작가, 이야기를 잘 하는 사람
straight hair (모발이) 직모인
strange 이상한, 기묘한, 생소한
strawberry 딸기
streetlight 가로등
stress 스트레스, 압박
strike 치다, 일격 가하다, 파업
strip 길고 가느다란 조각
strong 강한, (커피 등이) 진한
structure 구조, 구조, 조직
struggle 애쓰다, 분투하다, 투쟁
stubborn 완고한, 고집센
student 학생
study 공부하다, 연구하다
stuff 재료, 요소, 내용
stun 깜짝 놀라게 하다
stupid 바보 같은, 어리석은
style 문체, 방법, 스타일
stylish 스마트한, 현대식의
subject 주제, 과목, (문법) 주어
subjective 주관적인
subsequently 그 후, 계속해서
substitute 대체하다, 대용물
success 성공
successful 성공한, 좋은 결과의
suddenly 갑자기, 느닷없이
suffer 괴로워하다, 경험하다
sugar 설탕, (화학) 당질
suggest 제안하다, 암시하다
sum up 요약하다
summarize 요약하다
summary 요약, 개요
sunflower 해바라기
sunglasses 색안경, 선글라스
sunlight 햇빛
sunrise 해돋이
suntanned 햇볕에 그을린 피부
supermarket 슈퍼마켓
supplement 보충, 보충하다

support 지탱(지지)하다, 원조
supporting sentence 보조 문장
suppose 가정하다, 추측하다
sure 틀림없는, 확신하고 있는
surface 표면, 외면
surgery 외과, 수술
surname 성 (=family name, last name)
surprised 놀란
survey 조사, 조사표, 관찰
survival 생존
suspect ~이 아닌가 의심하다
suspicious 의심스러운
sweet 귀여운, 달콤한, 감미로운, (사탕 등의) 단 것
swim 헤엄치다, 수영하다
switch 전환하다, 바꾸다
sword 검, 칼
symbolism 상징주의
symbolize 상징하다, 나타내다
symmetry 대칭
sympathetic 동정심 있는
synonym 동의어, 비슷한 말
synthesize 종합하다, 합성하다
system 계통, 조직, 방식

T

table 테이블, 식탁, 작업대
table tennis 탁구
tablespoon (tbs) 식탁용 스푼
tactile 촉각의
tadpole 올챙이
taekwondo 태권도
tail 꼬리
Take care! 잘 지내!
take place 발생하다, 일어나다
take notes 메모하다, 필기하다
talent 재능
talk 말하다, 서로 이야기하다
talk show 대담프로, 토크쇼
tall 키가 큰
task 일, 임무, 과제
task-based 과제 중심의
taste 맛, 취향, 기호, 맛보다
teach 가르치다, 훈련하다
teacher 선생, 교사
team 팀
teamwork 팀워크
technician (전문)기술자
technological 과학 기술의
technology 공업(과학) 기술
telepathy 정신감응, 텔레파시
telephone 전화
television 텔레비전
tell 말하다, 이야기하다
temperature 온도, 체온
template 서식 파일, 틀
tender 부드러운, 연한
tennis racket 테니스 라켓
tense 팽팽한, (문법) 시제
terminally ill 회생 가망이 없는
terrible 괴로운, 끔찍한
terrific 훌륭한
terrorism 테러리즘, 테러행위
test 시험, 시험하다
text 원문, 본문, 텍스트
text message 문자 메세지
textbook 교과서, 교재
than ~보다
thankful 감사하는
theatre 극장, 연극
theme 테마, 주제
then 다음으로, 그 때
therefore 그러므로, 따라서
thereupon 그래서, 그 결과
these days 요즈음
thick 두꺼운
thief 도둑
thin 얇은
thin-lipped 입술이 얇은
thing 물건, 물체, 일, 사항
think 생각하다, 사고하다
thirst 갈증
thirsty 목마른
thorough 철저한, 순전한
though 비록, ~에도 불구하고
thought 생각
thoughtful 생각이 깊은, 신중한, 인정 있는, 정성어린
thousand 1,000의, 천개의, 천명의
thread 실, 줄
threat 위협, 협박
throne 왕좌, 왕위
throughout ~을 통하여, 도처에
throw 던지다, 내던지다, 팽개치다
thumb 엄지손가락
thunder 천둥
thus 이렇게, 따라서
tidal 조수의, 조력
tide 밀물, 조수, 시류
tights 스타킹
time 시간, 시각, 시간을 재다
time capsule 타임 캡슐
time-machine 타임 머신
time-management 시간관리
time-travel 시간 여행
timing 타이밍, 시간측정
tiny 작은, 조그마한
tip 팁, 힌트, 조언
tire 타이어
tired 피곤한, 지친
tissue 조직, 직물, 화장지
title 제목
tobacco 담배
today 오늘, 금일, 현재
toe 발가락
tomato 토마토
tomorrow 내일
too ~도 역시, 너무(나)
tools 도구, 수단
tooth 치아, 이빨
toothbrush 칫솔
toothpaste 치약
top 꼭대기, 맨 위, 최고의
topic 토픽, 논제, 화제
total 전체의, 합계의, 완전한
touch 만지다, ~에 닿다
tourism 관광 사업, 관광 여행
tournament 경기대회, 토너먼트
towel 수건
town 도회지, 지방의 중심지
track 통로, 선로, 궤도, 행로
tradition 전통
traditional 전통적인
traffic accident 교통사고
traffic light 통 신호등
traffic jam 교통 체증
train 열차, 기차
trainers 운동화
transition 전환, 연결
transportation 운송교통기관
trash bag 쓰레기 봉투
travel 여행, 여행하다
tread 걷다, 짓밟다
treasure 보물, 귀중품

treat 다루다, 한턱 내다
tree 나무
triangle 삼각형
trouble 근심, 괴로움
true 진실한, 진정한
trust 신뢰하다, 믿다
trustworthy 신뢰할 수 있는
truthful 거짓말 안하는, 진실의
try 노력하다, 시도하다
Tuesday 화요일
tuition fee 수업료, 등록금
turbine (기계) 터빈 엔진
turn 회전, 순번, 차례
twenty questions 스무고개
twice 두 번, 두 배로
type 유형
typhoon 태풍
typical 전형적인

U

UK (United Kingdom) 영국
umbrella 우산
uncomfortable 불편한
under 아래에(의), ~밑에(의)
underdeveloped 저개발의
underline 밑줄 긋다, 강조하다
understanding 이해심 있는
underwater 물 속의
uneasy 불안한
unfortunate 불운한, 불행한
unhappy 불행한, 즐겁지 않은
unique 독특한, 유일무이한
unit (교재의) 단원
unity (문단의) 통일성, 일관성
university 대학
unless ~하지 않으면
unlike 같지 않은, ~와 달리
unnecessary 불필요한
unselfish 이기적이 아닌, 욕심(사심) 없는
until ~까지, ~할 때까지
unusual 유별난, 진기한
up ~의 위로, ~위에
upper case letters 대문자
upset 뒤집어엎다, 당황케 하다, (마음의) 동요, 혼란
upside-down 거꾸로, 뒤집혀
uranium 우라늄
US, USA (United States of America) 미국
use 사용하다
useful 유용한, 쓸모 있는
user 사용자
usually 보통
ultra- 초~, 극단의, 최첨단의
UV (ultra-violet) 자외선

V

Valencia (스페인) 발렌시아
value 가치
valve 판, 밸브, 진공관
various 다양한, 각양각색의
vegetable 야채, 채소
vehicles 수송수단, 매개물
Venice (이탈리아) 베니스
venue (행사, 회의) 개최지
verb (품사) 동사
verbal 말의, 구두의, 말에 의한
very 매우, 바로 그
viewer (텔레비젼) 시청자
village 마을
virus (의학) 바이러스, 병균
visit 방문하다
visual 시각의, 시각에 호소하는 것 (사진, 도표 등)
visual aids (빔프로젝터, 비디오, 슬라이드 등의) 시각 기자재
vitamin 비타민
vocabulary 어휘
voice 목소리, 음성
volcano 화산
volume 음량, 볼륨
volunteer 지원자, 자발적인, 자발적으로 하다, 지원하다
voting 투표, 선거

W

wait 기다리다, 대기하다
walk 걷다, 산책
wall 벽
walnut 호두
want 원하다, 필요로 하다
war 전쟁
warm 따뜻한
warm-hearted 마음씨가 따뜻한, 온정적인, 친절한
wash 씻다, 씻어내다, 세탁하다
waste 쓰레기, 낭비하다
watch 지켜보다, 살펴보다
watch out 조심, 주의하다
water 물, 수분
water pollution 수질 오염
watermelon 수박
wavy 파도치는, 물결같은
way 방법, 길
way of thinking 사고방식
weak 약한, 의지력이 약한
wealth 부, 재산
wear 입고 있다
weather 날씨
Wednesday 수요일
week 주
weekend 주말
weigh 무게를 달다, 비교 고찰하다
welcome 환영하다, 환영
well 잘, 훌륭하게
well-managed 잘 관리된
well-organized 잘 짜여진
well-prepared 준비가 잘된
west 서쪽, 서양(the West)
wheat (곡류) 밀
wheel 바퀴
when 언제, ~할 때
whenever ~할 때마다
whereas ~임에 반하여
wherefore 무슨 이유로, 왜
whether ~인지 어떤지
which 어느, 어느 쪽
while-reading 독서중의
white 흰색, 화이트
white man 백인
whole 전체, 전체의
wide 넓은
wife 아내
wind 바람, 강풍
windmill 풍차
wine 와인, 포도주
winter 겨울
wire 철사, 전선, 전보
wireless 무선의
wisdom 지혜

wise 현명한, 지혜로운
wish upon a star 별을 보며 소원빌다
wish 소망, 바라다
within ~의 안쪽에, ~이내에, ~의 범위 안에
without ~없이, ~하지 않고
witty 재치 있는, 기지 있는
women 여자들, 여성들
wonderful 멋진, 훌륭한
wood 나무, 나무로 된
wooden spoon 나무 숟가락
word stress 단어 강세
work 작업, 일
workbook 워크북, 학습장
worker 일(공부)하는 사람, 노동자
worksheet 연습 문제지
world 세계, 지구
worldly 세상의, 세속적인
worried 걱정스러운
worse ~보다 나쁜, 악화된
wound 부상, 상처내다
wrestling 레슬링
wrist 손목
write 쓰다, 적다, 기록하다
writer 저자, 필자, 작가
writing 쓰기, 저작, 작품
wrong 잘못된, 틀린, 그릇된
www (컴퓨터) World Wide Web

y

year 연, 해, 연령, 학년
yearn 동경하다, 갈망하다
yellow 노란, 황색의
yesterday 어제
yet 아직 (~않다), 그러나
yogurt 요구르트(=yoghurt)
young 젊은, 어린, 새로운
yourself 당신 자신, 자기 자신

Answer Section (Units 1 to 3)

Unit 1 Quiz corner (▸page 6)

Q: What is the 4th child's name? A: Mary

Q: Who is speaking about whom? A: A father is speaking about his son.

Q: How many boys and girls in the family? A: 4 boys, 3 girls

Q: Who is asleep on your couch? A: Your father.

Unit 2 Quiz corner (▸page 18)

Q: What building has the most stories? A: A library

Q: What city has no people? A: Electricity

Q: What kind of clothes does a house wear? A: Address (A dress)

Q: What gets wetter as it dries? A: A towel

Unit 2 Capitals (▸page 19)

C C C C C
1. hello. my name is charles. i come from tunisia.

C C C C
2. dr. foster went to washington last tuesday.

C C C C C C
3. every time i visit seoul i go to the kimchi museum.

C C C C C
4. my favorite movie is called the matrix. keanu reeves is the main star.

C C
5. every sentence starts with a capital letter. proper nouns have capitals too.

Unit 3 Punctuation and Capitalization (▸page 31)

period	.	hyphen	-	exclamation mark	!
comma	,	asterisk	*	apostrophe	'
colon	:	question mark	?	parentheses	( )
semicolon	;	quotation marks	" "	square brackets	[ ]

1. Michael is a student in UCLA.
2. Is Central Park in the USA?
3. Mr. Smith said, "Come here at once!"
4. The capital of England is London, isn't it?
5. A man chooses; a slave obeys.
6. Excuse me. Where's the station?
7. I'm visiting these places: Paris, France; Berlin, Germany; and Rome, Italy.

Answer Section (Units 3 to 5)

Unit 3 **Quiz corner** (▸page 31)

You are driving a bus. Four people get on and three people get off. Then eight people get on and ten people get off. Then six people get on and two more people get off. What color are the bus driver's eyes?

Q: What color are the bus driver's eyes?

A: What color are your eyes? You are driving the bus.

Unit 4 **Apostrophes and personal pronouns** (▸page 44)

Subject	Object	Apostrophe	Adjective	Possessive
I	me	I'm happy	my	mine
you	you	You're happy	your	yours
he	him	He's happy	his	his
she	her	She's happy	her	hers
we	us	We're happy	our	ours
they	them	They're happy	their	theirs

1. That's not my dog. I'm certain about that.
2. It's too late to visit her now. She's probably asleep.
3. We're going to Frank's party in our cars.
4. Today's trip is our first holiday this year. It's a beautiful day.
5. The women's soccer players had their first game today.
6. The children's toys are in their boxes.
7. This isn't their house. It's mine. That's theirs over there.

Unit 5 **My festivals** (▸page 49)

12	Mardi Gras	2	Edinburgh Festival	7	Boryeong Mud Festival
11	Rio Carnival	9	Cape Town Festival	8	Melbourne Arts Festival
3	Oktoberfest	4	Ice Lantern Festival	13	Valencia Tomato Festival
6	HiSeoul Festival	1	Notting Hill Carnival	15	Montreal Jazz Festival
14	Festival d'Avignon	5	Sapporo Snow Festival	10	Marrakech Popular Arts Festival

Answer Section (Units 5 to 6)

Unit 5 Singular/plural, Count/non-count (▶page 55)

1. Everyone has finished their work.
2. None of them has eaten much meat.
3. I spread some butter on the slices of bread.
4. There was little time to listen to any music.
5. We have had lots of extreme weather recently.
6. There were a few pieces of furniture in the room.
7. It takes a lot of courage to fight for your beliefs.
8. None of the guests drank any wine.
9. Do you drink enough water each day?
10. Which is more important, leisure or education?

Unit 5 Quiz corner (▶page 55)

1. What is in the middle of Paris? **A:** The letter 'r'.
2. How long was the 100 years war? **A:** It lasted 116 years, from 1337 to 1453.
3. What happened in 1961 and will not happen again until 6009?
   A: 1961 and 6009 have rotational symmetry; they look the same when rotated through 180°.

Unit 5 Writing skills (▶page 56)

Track 21

Best Friends

Tom and Tim have been friends for a long time, so they have many things in common. For example, they both like music and movies and they are both morning people. Then again, they also have their differences. For one thing, Tom is left-handed and easy-going, unlike Tim, who is right-handed and quick-tempered. For another thing, Tom has brown eyes and short, fair hair, whereas Tim is blue-eyed and curly-haired. Tim is also taller than Tom, and more athletic. He likes all sports. Tom, on the other hand, is rather flat-footed and prefers to read a book or ride his bike.

Unit 6 My myths (▶page 61)

1. Achilles' heel	2. Ariadne's thread	3. Cupid's arrow	4. Hercules' tasks
5. Icarus' wings	6. Medusa's head	7. Midas' hand	8. Minotaur's maze
9. Odysseus' adventure	10. Oedipus complex	11. Pandora's box	12. Prometheus' fire
13. Sisyphus' stone			

Unit 6 Legends in their own lifetime (▶page 65)

1. Park Ji-sung	2. Gandhi	3. Kim Yu-na
4. Nelson Mandela	5. Vincent van Gogh	6. Ban Ki-moon

Answer Section (Units 6 to 7)

Unit 6 Spelling (▸page 67)

Sp Sp
Angela's Dairy, April twelth
Diary twelfth

Sp Sp
The whether was fine this after-noon so I had a walk in the
weather afternoon

Sp Sp Gr1 Sp Sp
prak. I often go there accept when its rainning and sometime
park except it's raining sometimes

Sp Gr1 Sp Sp
I stay untill evening. Its not to far and the exercize does me
until It's too exercise

Sp Sp Sp
good. Toady I met my nieghbor, Janice. She has been unwel, but
Today neighbor unwell

Sp Sp Sp Sp
to-day she looked very helthy. We gossipped for housr as we
today healthy gossiped hours

Sp Sp Sp Sp
wondered thrugh the treees and sharred our news.
wandered through trees shared

Unit 6 Spelling (▸page 67)

✗ beleive	✓ believe
exceed	✗ excede
✗ independant	✓ independent
US judgment	UK judgement
UK licence	US license
✓ receive	✗ recieve

✓ calendar	✗ calender
✗ greatful	✓ grateful
✗ accomodation	✓ accommodation
✗ liesure	✓ leisure
✓ pastime	✗ pasttime
✓ schedule	✗ scedule

Unit 7 Quiz corner (▸page 78)

1. Q: What is the answer to this multiplication problem?
   A: 111,111,111 X 111,111,111 = 12,345,678,987,654,321
2. Q: What are two things you cannot eat for dinner?
   A: Breakfast and lunch.

Answer Section (Units7 to 8)

Unit 7 Prepositions (▸page 79)

Track 31

First of all, you need to go to the Virtual Language Centre site online. You can find this at http://vlc.polyu.edu.hk. This is a free site. You don't have to log in. When the page loads, you will see a box in the center of the screen. Above the box are the words "Research and Reference." Underneath these words, at the top of the box, are the words "Web Concordancer." Below are three white boxes to the right, and the word "keyword" to the left. If you click on the arrow in the "equal to" box, the words "starts with," "ends with," and "contains," appear. When you are looking for a word or phrase, you can choose one of these options. Then you enter your search word or phrase in the box on the right, and click on "Go." Then you will see a screen with your search item in the middle of the page, in blue, surrounded by black text. This is a good way of finding collocations and seeing a word or phrase as it is used in real life.

Unit 8 Quiz corner (▸page 90)

Q: What is the smallest number of actions?

A: Your hand only needs to touch one glass and to make one action. Pick up glass number 2 (the middle one of the three full glasses), pour the water into glass number 5 (the middle one of the empty glasses) and put glass 2 back between glasses 1 and 3.

Unit 8 Articles (▸page 91)

Track 36

Going through Customs and Immigration Control

When you travel by air to a foreign country, there is a process that you have to follow before you can board the plane. On arrival at the airport, the first thing you need to do is to check-in and get a boarding pass. Once you have your boarding pass you can proceed to the security check. After you have been through security you come to the customs control, where your passport is checked. You are now free to enter the departure lounge, while you wait to board your flight. In order to complete the whole process in time, it is a good idea to arrive at the airport at least two hours before your flight takes off.

1. I went to the Island of Dokdo and had the time of my life.
2. The Queen of England understands the value of education.
3. The President of France spoke about the benefits of technology.
4. He is The Speaker of The House of Representatives.
5. The joy of being alive is at the top of my list of good things.

1. Beethoven was a famous composer. (famous/a famous/the famous)
2. This is not a difficult question. (difficult/a difficult/the difficult)
3. She speaks French well. (French/a French/the French)
4. We had very good weather last week. (very/a very/the very)
5. She is in good health for an 80-year old. (good/a good/the good)
6. He comes from Texas. (Texas/the Texas)
7. Mount Hallasan is the highest in Korea. (Mount/A Mount/The Mount)
8. A spider is not an insect. (Spider/A spider/The spider)(insect/an insect/the insect)

Answer Section (Units 8 to 9)

Unit 8 The process paragraph (1) (▸page 92)

Title	Making Paper
Topic sentence	We use paper every day, but do we know how it is made?
Body sentence 1	First, trees used for papermaking are harvested, the bark is removed and the trees are cut into 1-inch pieces.
Body sentence 2	These are boiled in water and chemicals, and the resulting pulp is washed and pumped onto a moving wire screen.
Body sentence 3	The water drains away and the new paper sheet is squeezed between two rollers.
Body sentence 4	After it has dried, the finished paper is wound onto rolls.
Conclusion sentence	Large papermaking machines can make up to 1,000 miles of paper a day.

Unit 9 Discoveries and inventions (▸page 97)

1. Satellites
2. The printing press
3. Television
4. Clocks
5. The automobile
6. Mobile phones
7. The Internet, Computers
8. Airplanes

Unit 9 Writing workshop (▸page 103)

1. The soccer team practices in the gym every day.
2. Most people like to see a good movie.
3. He doesn't like horror movies.
4. Mary and her friends have gone shopping.
5. One of the books has disappeared

The Advantages and Disadvantages of Fast Food

I likes [S/v] (like) fast food because it are [S/v] (is) very convenient. The main advantage are [S/v] (is) that it save [S/v] (saves) time. I can eats [S/v] (eat) immediately at fast food restaurants, whereas when I cooks [S/v] (cook) at home I have to buys [S/v] (buy) the ingredients, prepares [S/v] (prepare) them, and cooks [S/v] (cook) the meal. Another advantage are [S/v] (is) that fast foods like burgers and fries is [S/v] (are) quite cheap, while others, like salads and whole-grain bread rolls, is [S/v] (are) also healthy.

However, there is [S/v] (are) also disadvantages. Fast food contain [S/v] (contains) more salt, fats and calories than home-cooked meals. Because of this, it can causes [S/v] (cause) obesity. In addition, many families spends [S/v] (spend) less time eating together. We needs [S/v] (need) to thinks [S/v] (think) about the pros and cons of fast food and makes [S/v] (make) sure we eats [S/v] (eat) a balanced diet.

Answer Section (Units 10 to 11)

Unit 10 Writing workshop (▸page 115)

1. Does she | every week | play table tennis?
   Does she play table tennis every week?
2. We're going | on Tuesday | to visit her.
   We're going to visit her on Tuesday.
3. For a long time | they were married.
   They were married for a long time.
4. I | want | really | to speak | well | English.
   I really want to speak English well.
5. Jeremy | walks | always | to school.
   Jeremy always walks to school.
6. She is | only | the | person who can | this puzzle | solve.
   She is the only person who can solve this puzzle.

Unit 11 Presentation Dos and Don'ts (▸page 130)

1. MAKE EYE CONTACT
2. FINISH LATE
3. FACE THE AUDIENCE
4. SMART CLOTHES
5. SPEAK CLEARLY
6. REMEMBER YOUR SPEECH
7. ARRIVE LATE
8. USE FLASH CARDS
9. PREPARE EVERYTHING
10. KEEP IT SIMPLE
11. REHEARSE OFTEN
12. ASK FOR QUESTIONS
13. AUDIOVISUAL AIDS
14. FINISH ON TIME
15. BE PROFESSIONAL
16. ALWAYS SMILE
17. HESITATE AND MUMBLE
18. BE CONFIDENT
19. BEGIN ON TIME

1	2	3	4	5	6	7	8	9	10
✓	✗	✓	✓	✓	✓	✗	✓	✓	✓

11	12	13	14	15	16	17	18	19
✓	✓	✓	✓	✓	✓	✗	✓	✓

Plan of writing process and assignments

Week	Unit	In class		Homework		
Week 1	UNIT 1	E-mail writing in class. Personal introduction One draft only			→	
Week 2	UNIT 2	Listing paragraph, draft 1, peer-editing in class	→	Homework (Unit 2) final draft	→	
Week 3	UNIT 3	Description paragraph, draft 1, peer-editing in class	→	Homework (Unit 3) draft 2	→	teacher
Week 4	UNIT 4	Order of importance paragraph, draft 1, peer-editing in class	→	Homework (Unit 4) final draft	→	
Week 5	UNIT 5	Teacher returns Unit 3 2nd draft, with feedback	→	Homework (Unit 3) final draft	→	
		Comparison/contrast paragraph, draft 1, peer-editing in class	→	Homework (Unit 5) final draft	→	
Week 6	UNIT 6	Time order paragraph, draft 1 Peer-editing in class	→	Homework (Unit 6) draft 2	→	teacher
Week 7	UNIT 7	'How to' paragraph, draft 1, peer-editing in class	→	Homework (Unit 7) final draft	→	
Week 8		Teacher returns Unit 6 2nd draft, with feedback	→	Homework (Unit 6) final draft	→	
		Mid-term Test				
Week 9	UNIT 8	Process paragraph, draft 1 Peer-editing in class	→	Homework (Unit 8) final draft	→	
Week 10	UNIT 9	Advantage/disadvantage paragraphs, draft 1, peer-editing in class	→	Homework (Unit 9) final draft	→	
Week 11	UNIT 10	Cause and effect paragraph, draft 1, peer-editing in class	→	Homework (Unit 10) final draft	→	
Week 12	UNIT 11	Presentations skills; Structure; Language focus; Four stages				
Week 13	UNIT 11	Students plan and prepare their presentations in class. The teacher gives help and feedback where needed.				
Week 14	UNIT 11	Students prepare and practice their presentations in class. The teacher gives help and feedback where needed.				
Week 15		Final Test: Presentations				